THE POPE

Anthony McCarten

THE POPE

OBERON BOOKS
LONDON

WWW.OBERONBOOKS.COM

First published in 2019 by Oberon Books Ltd
521 Caledonian Road, London N7 9RH
Tel: +44 (0) 20 7607 3637 / Fax: +44 (0) 20 7607 3629
e-mail: info@oberonbooks.com
www.oberonbooks.com

A catalogue record for this book is available from the British Library.

PB ISBN: 9781786827869
E ISBN: 9781786827852

Cover design: Tom McCarten

Visit www.oberonbooks.com to read more about all our books and to buy them. You will
also find features, author interviews and news of any author events, and you can sign up for
e-newsletters so that you're always first to hear about our new releases.

10 9 8 7 6 5 4 3 2 1

Characters

POPE BENEDICT
(Aka JOSEPH RATZINGER)

CARDINAL BERGOGLIO
(The future POPE FRANCIS)

SISTER BRIGITTA
(A German Nun, and book editor)

SISTER SOPHIA
(A 30 year old Argentinian Nun)

*This edition went to print before the first performance
and therefore the text may contain some differences.*

ACT 1

PROLOGUE

Over darkness, the stage is flooded with the image of many lit candles, a night-sky of small single flickering points of light. (Single candles may even have been dispersed and be burning in the hands of the audience.)

Soft Choral music is heard, befitting a cathedral choir, singing in Latin...

The tranquil mood is exploded when –

– a) a church organ blasts a single discordant note – and, at the same moment –

– b) a spot light (from directly above) snaps on, illuminating the DEAD BODY of POPE JOHN PAUL II, centre stage, on either his death-bed or a plinth. The body is flanked by two tall ceremonial candles.

The POPE IS DEAD!

(Two altar attendants or nuns, if possible, enter and, with brass candle 'snuffers', put out the flames.) All candles throughout the auditorium to go out at this point.

Lights down on this scene, as we –

– transition into a cacophany of human voices (with images, projected, or otherwise indicated) signifying 120 CARDINALS in CONCLAVE in the SISTINE CHAPEL, voting for the new pope. Much debate as to who should be the next pope...

White Smoke (from a Vatican chimney or otherwise) indicates that a NEW POPE HAS BEEN CHOSEN...

The scene and mood smoothly change to...

...one of CELEBRATION. It's now a bright, sunny morning...

THREE sets of PAPAL ROBES, on a mobile clothes rack, await the new pope – one very small, one medium-sized, one very large.

Date: 19 April, 2005. A new POPE has been elected.

We are now in the "Room of Tears", the room in the Basilica backing the famous balcony that overlooks the Square Of St Peter, from which countless Popes have appeared to address the massed faithful.

Enter, the new POPE, POPE BENEDICT XVI (78), stepping into a bolt of heavenly light from above, as if falling under the eye of God – the chosen one.

We hear (OFF-STAGE, from the balcony), the voice of the PROTODEACON speaking to the crowds:

PROTODEACON *(OFF.)*: Fratelli e sorelle carissimi *(Italian.)*

As the PROTODEACON proceeds with his speech…

…the new POPE is dressed in the robes of office by TWO ATTENDANTS or NUNS… the RED ROBE/CASSOCK with ERMINE COLLAR, the MITRE, the PAPAL FERULA (staff), and finally, the RED SHOES.

During this…

PROTODEACON *(OFF.)*: Queridísimos hermanos y hermanas. *(Spanish.)*

(The crowd roars.)

Bien chers frères et soeurs. *(French.)*

(The crowd roars.)

Liebe Brüder und Schwestern. *(German.)*

(The crowd roars.)

Queridos irmãos e irmãs *(Portugese.)*

(The crowd roars.)

Ndugu na dada wapendwa *(Swahili.)*

(The crowd roars.)

Agapitoí adelfoí kai adelfés *(Greek.)*

(The crowd roars.)

Qin'ài de xiongdì jiemèimen *(Chinese.)*

(The crowd roars.)

Dear brothers and sisters.

I announce to you a great joy.

Annuntio vobis gaudium magnum:

HABEMUS...PAPAM!

(The crowd roars.)

WE HAVE...A POPE!

The BELLS of ROME ring out.

POPE BENEDICT: *(To the audience.)* The "Room of Tears." How many popes have wept in this moment?

Meanwhile...

PROTODEACON *(OFF.)*: *(The crowd roars.)* Eminentissimum ac reverendissimum Dominum,

The Most Eminent and Reverend Lord,

Dominum Ratzinger,

Lord Ratzinger,

Sanctæ Romanæ Ecclesiæ Cardinalem Munchen,

Cardinal of the Holy Roman Church, Munich,

We hear THREE RAPS on the DOORS UPSTAGE (that lead out to the famous balcony overlooking St Peter's Square).

POPE BENEDICT *turns and faces the DOUBLE DOORS to the great balcony. He cannot yet be seen by the people outside in the square.*

PROTODEACON *(OFF.)*: Qui sibi nomen imposuit...

The moment has arrived: Finally the new POPE walks toward the doors...

PROTODEACON *(OFF.)*: ...BENEDICT !

POPE BENEDICT: At a certain point, I prayed to God 'please don't do this to me'...Evidently, this time he didn't listen to me.

The DOUBLE DOORS open at last. A column of LIGHT enters the room.

Here, we switch the location of the balcony and the waiting crowd 180 degrees...

...so that the THEATRE AUDIENCE now becomes the crowd.

The new POPE therefore moves DOWNSTAGE, following the column of light, coming to the forward edge of the stage, and as he does so we hear the roar of the crowd...

(Production note: Behind the POPE – the scene begins, in darkness, to change in preparation for Scene One.)

A mighty roar, as he steps out onto the 'balcony', facing the theatre audience. He raises his arms in celebration and acknowledgement. Finally he raises his right hand to silence the tens of thousands... and the crowd dutifully falls silent...

POPE BENEDICT: Vos, dilecti Fratres et Sorores, Postquam Pontifex Ioannes Paulus II, cardinales creati me simplices, humiles operarius in vinea Domini...

(PROJECT SUR-TITLES.)

Dear Brothers and Sisters, After the great Pope John Paul II, the Cardinals have elected me a simple humble worker in the Lord's vineyard.

SNAP TO BLACK

SCENE 1

A stormy night in Rome, rain beating down heavily, occasional lightning and thunder…

We are now in the modest convent apartment of a nun, SISTER BRIGITTA. The room is simply but comfortably furnished – it is homely, comforting. Specifically, the room has a PIANO and a TV and a small cooking appliance, a TABLE, on which a MEAL has been set (two bowls covered with steel lids) and TWO CHAIRS.

SISTER BRIGITTA, a German nun, is currently trying to get some reception on her little set-top TV/SATELLITE aerial. The picture ghosts… comes and goes…but with a little work it should be possible to watch a program.

When a knock sounds on the door, she turns the TV off, and goes to open the door…

Enter POPE BENEDICT, dressed in a black coat and a green Tyrolean hat…as if he wished to be incognito, shaking water off a BLACK UMBRELLA.

He also carries a VALISE heavy with papers. She assists him with his UMBRELLA, his HAT, his COAT.

SISTER BRIGITTA: Euer Heiligkeit! Komm herein, komm herein! Servus. Servus.

POPE BENEDICT: Servus. Servus Schwester. Servus Schwester. Wie gehts? Alles gut?

SISTER BRIGITTA: Ja, ja!
    Dein Mantel *(Coat.)*
    Lassen Sie mich Ihren
    Mantel. Unt Hat. *(Hat.)*
    Oh,oh,oh…

POPE BENEDICT: Toll, toll.
    Ah…Such rain. Not since
    Noah…not since the Book
    Of Genesis…

SISTER BRIGITTA: Ja. Ja. It is a deluge. A flood.

POPE BENEDICT: I didn't know whether to come here…or to build an ark.

A loud rumble of THUNDER. The POPE only now notices that the TV is on, the screen snowy with static –

POPE BENEDICT: *(Concerned.)* Dear God! The TV! Will the storm effect the signal?

SISTER BRIGITTA: We must pray. It comes from a satellite so I think we are fine.

POPE BENEDICT: Satellites move in mysterious ways. How long do we have before it starts?

SISTER BRIGITTA: We have time.

POPE BENEDICT: I can barely think of anything else this past week than the fate of our little German shepherd. Little Rex.

The POPE is still holding his VALISE. She offers to take it –

SISTER BRIGITTA: Deiner Tascher *(Valise.)*?

POPE BENEDICT: Oh. Good news.

He opens the VALISE and takes out a 500 PAGES OF UNBOUND MANUSCRIPT…

POPE BENEDICT: Sister. Good news. I have made a very good beginning…on the manuscript…on your edits to our third volume.

As the POPE holds up the MANUSCRIPT, the NUN is shocked and concerned by this news.

SISTER BRIGITTA: How…but how did you find the time? Your holiness –

POPE BENEDICT: It is my highest priority.

SISTER BRIGITTA: Highest? At such a time? Of crisis? Your holiness –

POPE BENEDICT: It is vital I release the third volume.

He holds out the MANUSCRIPT to her:

POPE BENEDICT: See. Look how much progress I made. Almost finished.

But she refuses at first to take it…

POPE BENEDICT: Sister. I got up to page 455.

SISTER BRIGITTA: Holy Father, is this the best use of your time? With so much upheaval?

She takes the MANUSCRIPT at last, and looks through some pages… and each are FULL OF NOTES/ANNOTATIONS/SCRIBBLES…

SISTER BRIGITTA: Every page! Full of your notes, corrections!

POPE BENEDICT: I became obsessed.

SISTER BRIGITTA: Holy Father, forgive me, forgive me for saying so, but this…this is exactly what your enemies accuse you of –

POPE BENEDICT: What enemies?

SISTER BRIGITTA: Those who say you are detached, spending hours and hours with your head in your books, writing, reading, not focused enough on your daily papal duties, when your church requires strong leadership, especially now. I want to assist you, holy father, protect you from this criticism. Your third volume on the life of Jesus Of Nazareth is a valuable document, but others must see your qualities of leadership which I know you possess, feel your great authority and wisdom and learning, to guide the church through –

POPE BENEDICT: Please. *Enough!*

When he covers his ear with his hand she realises she has over-stepped the mark, and annoyed him.

POPE BENEDICT: *(Softer.)* Enough sister. Please, I beg you. I'm exhausted. I came to eat with you…to show you my hard work, of which I thought you'd be proud, apparently not… and to distract myself with a little TV.

She puts the MANUSCRIPT down, and bows her head in supplication.

SISTER BRIGITTA: Forgive me.

POPE BENEDICT: This…our third volume…will enhance greatly the first two, you'll see. It will put the cat among the pigeons. *(Smiles.)* It may be my most important contribution. Now then, remind me…about our little dog, where we got up to last week? Ha! Ha! What trouble he gets into each week! When I think I have worries with all this Vatican business, with the fate of the world, I think of little Rex – a dog tasked with so much.

SISTER BRIGITTA: But first, Holy Father, while I serve the food, you play. Play. Please. It brings you peace.

POPE BENEDICT: Ah yes. Play…

BENEDICT looks at the PIANO and limbers up his fingers.

POPE BENEDICT: …a word from another time, another age… Play. To have idle hours…to have nothing to do…

SISTER BRIGITTA: And then we eat. Suppe. Your favorite.

POPE BENEDICT: Suppe.

(Hopeful.)

Mit Knoedel?

SISTER BRIGITTA: Mit Knoedel! Fresh. Ten different herbs from the Black Forest.

POPE BENEDICT begins to open the MUSIC books stacked on the PIANO, looking for something by MOZART...passing over the other great composers...

POPE BENEDICT: Ahhh. How my brother and I used to die...Bach...waiting for mother to pour the soup over the Knoedel... Brahms... Beethoven... Then, to cut into it with our eager little spoons, heaven! Mozart! Here we go!

POPE BENEDICT selects this BOOK of sheet-music and sets it on the stand and leafs through it...

He begins to play his beloved Mozart – Piano Concerto No 27.

SISTER BRIGITTA stops her preparation of the Knoedel to listen to the POPE play. He plays very well, but his playing is not without error...which annoys him...

POPE BENEDICT: Oh!

SISTER BRIGITTA: Sehr gut...Euer Heiligkeit...

He repeats the section...managing to play it better but once again coming unstuck...

POPE BENEDICT: ...scheiße... Forgive me. *(for the swear-word or the playing it's not clear!)*

Finally his fingers flow again, but there is a halting hesitancy to his playing today, as SISTER BRIGITTA, goes back to her meal preparations. The PONTIFF plays on, until...he finishes...mid phrase...takes his hands from the keys...looks at the keys in frustration and then re-sets his fingers over the keys...

...but this time he plays a rolling (New Orleans) BOOGIE WOOGIE!!! ...

SISTER BRIGITTA is shocked. The POPE turns and looks at her as he plays, showing no expression, but he is aware he is being controversial.

He finishes and stands, looking at her.

SISTER BRIGITTA returns to her food preparations...

POPE BENEDICT: I am not in the mood today. I can't play anymore. Even Mozart has forsaken me. Too much going on... *(points to his head)*...but I do like to come here. It is one of the few places I can truly relax. But it is getting extremely difficult to avoid the paparazzi. My driver had to lose them on the Via Julia.

SISTER BRIGITTA: Sehr gut...Euer Heiligkeit...

POPE BENEDICT: But I think I was recognized by tourists, coming up the stairs. Tourists, in a convent! I don't think they got a picture in time.

SISTER BRIGITTA: But for the tourists, your holiness – we could not financially survive.

POPE BENEDICT: How many nuns remain in the convent, sister?

SISTER BRIGITTA: When I started there were 90.

POPE BENEDICT: 90!

SISTER BRIGITTA: Now we are 15 – mostly African and Indian sisters. And many are very old – the oldest is 94.

POPE BENEDICT: New novices?

Pause –

SISTER BRIGITTA: This year?

POPE BENEDICT: Yes. How many new novices?

SISTER BRIGITTA: One. Chinese. How do you have a class with one novice?

POPE BENEDICT: It is true. Any number less than two does not constitute a religious community –

SISTER BRIGITTA: – as the term is defined under doctrine. But the young in Italy have TV. They have cell phones. They have these laptops they carry around. When you are going to discos, how can you expect to hear the word of God? You need silence to hear God.

POPE BENEDICT: Bless you, sister.

SISTER BRIGITTA: When families were larger they were more likely to send one to the convent. We could rely on the quiet one of the family being dropped off at our door. Now? The well has run dry. Even the quiet ones have Facebook and 2000 so-called "*friends.*"

POPE BENEDICT: Yes. The industrialization of friendship.

SISTER BRIGITTA: Forgive me your holiness for expressing such fears.

POPE BENEDICT: No. I am afflicted by the decay of numbers every day. It is a mark of our failure to awaken in the young a hunger for the truth. This is the gravest crisis. We must halt this erosion.

SISTER BRIGITTA: With God's grace you will do it.

The POPE picks up a picture of a young man.

POPE BENEDICT: You never told me who this handsome young man is?

SISTER BRIGITTA: You never asked.

POPE BENEDICT: I look at this photo every time I come here.

SISTER BRIGITTA: Just…

POPE BENEDICT: Just?

SISTER BRIGITTA: An old friend.

POPE BENEDICT: An old boyfriend?

SISTER BRIGITTA: No, no, no, no, no.

He puts down the photo, and becomes wistful…

POPE BENEDICT: You told me you once had a boyfriend.

SISTER BRIGITTA: Oh yes. For about a year. I was very happy and thought that we might get married in the end. That relationship was immensely important. Maybe I wouldn't have entered religious life without that. It's not that it broke my heart, but it showed me how great my heart is and therefore how great my capacity for God is.

(Forgetting herself.)

Did you ever have a girlfriend?

He stares at her.

SISTER BRIGITTA: Forgive me, Holy father.

POPE BENEDICT: We are friends…

SISTER BRIGITTA: I don't know why I said that.

POPE BENEDICT: No. No girlfriends. Well…there was one. Her mother was a wonderful baker. In the playground this girl used to let me…pick…the salt off her pretzel. That was it. That's as close at it ever got. My talents lay elsewhere.

(Pause.)

I preferred my large teddy-bear. I still have it. And I have Archbishop Ganswein, of course…it's 25 years now he has been my personal secretary.

SISTER BRIGITTA: That long?

POPE BENEDICT: So let us agree I will not rank among the most romantically experienced of popes!

SISTER BRIGITTA: What a thing. A romantically experienced pope!

POPE BENEDICT: St Peter himself had children. Clement IV and Adrian the Second were married before they took Holy Orders. Pius the Second had at least two illegitimate children. And let's just say Pope Innocent did not live up to his name!

SISTER BRIGITTA laughs!

POPE BENEDICT: Not to speak of those sexually active during their Pontificate. John the Twelfth is even said to have died in this way.

SISTER BRIGITTA: No!

POPE BENEDICT: Oh yes. In the act. And we dare not discuss the Borges. But these were men from a different age. By the nineteenth century we had our house in order. Celibacy re-instated.

(Gravely.)

Or so we thought.

The POPE sits again at the piano and begins to play the Concerto again, while the SISTER resumes setting the table…but then stops when new inner concerns halt the Pontiff's playing…

POPE BENEDICT: Age! Old age! I may be Pope, but my fingers are not infallible. I give up!

SISTER BRIGITTA: Then sit. I have a bottle…one bottle of Weisbier…

POPE BENEDICT: No, no. Thank you no.

She produces the bottle and holds it up, tempting him.

POPE BENEDICT: I must not. Get behind me Satan, ha!ha!

SISTER BRIGITTA: Would you mind awfully if I…?

POPE BENEDICT: I would object only if you did not. How many years have we known each other, Sister?

SISTER BRIGITTA: Eighteen years.

POPE BENEDICT: Your tolerance of me is a miracle and your assistance with my work invaluable. I wish only you had been able to remain my housekeeper when I moved into the Vatican.

SISTER BRIGITTA: It is my fault. One moment of weakness. But I saw no harm in it at the time.

POPE BENEDICT: It was human.

SISTER BRIGITTA: One little wave, from the balcony, to the faithful below in St Peters Square.

POPE BENEDICT: Human.

SISTER BRIGITTA: It was foolish. Vain. And I was not forgiven. Who did I think I was? A woman, standing in the Pope's place. How awful. God forgive me.

POPE BENEDICT: The rules. Rules are rules.

SISTER BRIGITTA sets out cutlery –

POPE BENEDICT: What times these are, sister. What times these are?

How many winds of doctrine we have known in recent decades, how many ideological currents…

SISTER BRIGITTA: How many new ways of thinking?

POPE BENEDICT: But who speaks the truth? What *is* the truth? Can everybody be in opposition and all be right? The town-hall quakes with rival voices – Marxists, liberals, conservatives, atheists, agnostics, mystics – and in every breast the universal cry: "I speak the truth!"

SISTER BRIGITTA: Sayeth the Lord, "I am the way, the truth…"

POPE BENEDICT: *(Passionately.)* There must be a common reference point! There must!

SISTER BRIGITTA: One. Yes.

POPE BENEDICT: One! Interpreted from many angles but one, fixed, unchanging, reliable truth from which we can all navigate. Away from and back toward. Take the traveller who is lost. He takes out a, what?

SISTER BRIGITTA: A mobile phone.

POPE BENEDICT: Call it a compass. In my day a compass … which? Which can point in all directions, but!…which takes at its starting point?

SISTER BRIGITTA: True North?

She points to his CHAIR, bidding him to be seated…

SISTER BRIGITTA: Your Holiness?

POPE BENEDICT: True North! Then what of human morality? What is *its* True North? Its *axis mundi*?

SISTER BRIGITTA: God.

POPE BENEDICT: Without God, humanity has no agreed reference point, no *axis mundi*. Every opinion is as valid as every other. The truth becomes *relative*. Do away with God and what you actually do away with is any hope of absolute truth. Your truth is yours, mine is mine, locking each person into a prison…the prison of his or her own interpretation of good and evil.

SISTER BRIGITTA: Come now, no time for old discredited ideas…Eat. While it's hot.

SISTER BRIGITTA again points at his CHAIR at the table. He finally crosses and sits.

She lifts the steel lids on two bowls of Knoedel mit Sosse…

POPE BENEDICT: That is the great crisis of Western life.

(Beat.)

And now?…fewer and fewer take their fire from the flame lit by a two thousand-year old faith, the Christian faith, which was also Plato's faith, that God is Truth; that Truth is 'Divine'.

(Smelling his food.)

Ah…

SISTER BRIGITTA: Eat. While it's hot.

POPE BENEDICT: The smell of a Bavarian forest after the rain.

(He makes the SIGN OF THE CROSS over the food and then they both begin to pray.)

POPE BENEDICT: Bless us Oh Lord, and these thy gifts, which we are about to receive…We thank you, for this food…and for my good friend's generosity in having it shipped…

SISTER BRIGITTA: By Fed Ex.

POPE BENEDICT: By Fed-Ex…from her village to this table… the product of her own family's care and love…

SISTER BRIGITTA: Amen.

SISTER BRIGITTA begins to "bless herself" with the Sign Of The Cross, and opens her eyes, thinking Grace completed...but she closes her eyes again as the POPE, eyes still closed, resumes...

POPE BENEDICT: ...so that we may enjoy it here...in this place...outside of time and the...the relentless concerns of the outside world...

(Silence – is the prayer over?)

...if but for a moment...serenity...peace...tranquility...

(Silence, then –)

Lord, our eternal *axis mundi*...your church, your flock is in crisis...Grant us.the wisdom...and the strength of body and mind in this time of great struggle... to...

(The POPE, eyes closed is under great strain, even suffering.)

...to reassert...*adequatio rei et intellectus*...the correspondence of the mind and reality...

(To SISTER BRIGITTA.)

Would you like to say something?

SISTER BRIGITTA: Amen ?

POPE BENEDICT: Amen.

They pick up their spoons to eat – SISTER BRIGITTA now very hesitant to eat before the Pontiff does...POPE BENEDICT looks at her.

POPE BENEDICT: You know, Sister, whenever a Pope eats, there used to be three Jesuits present to act as "food tasters." Lack of Jesuits has killed more than one pope.

SISTER BRIGITTA quickly dips her spoon into the soup and tastes the dish. The POPE is amused...

POPE BENEDICT: Ha! Well?

SISTER BRIGITTA: Perhaps a little salt?

They begin to eat, in silence – SISTER BRIGITTA clearly concerned for her friend.

POPE BENEDICT: Sehr gut. Delicious.

SISTER BRIGITTA smiles, as she opens her small bottle of beer...

POPE BENEDICT: Where were we?

SISTER BRIGITTA: Your holiness?

POPE BENEDICT: Last week. "Kommissar Rex."

SISTER BRIGITTA: Oh. How it ended? Awful. It ended with the kidnapper pointing his gun at Rex, finger tightening on the trigger!

POPE BENEDICT: Yes, I know!

SISTER BRIGITTA: ...then squeezing the trigger? Terrible, terrible. The gun-shot and then the screen went dark, and then the words... "*to be continued next week*".

POPE BENEDICT: Agony. Agony. Rex has been much in my prayers.

(Pause.)

You know I am often referred to as a –

SISTER BRIGITTA: – a dog? No, no, no, no.

POPE BENEDICT: "God's Rottweiler" – that is my nickname ... in the world's press.

SISTER BRIGITTA: No, no, no, one awful German newspaper perhaps.

POPE BENEDICT: "Panza Papst – the Panzer Pope."

SISTER BRIGITTA: Awful.

POPE BENEDICT: "God's Enforcer"…a cold theologian imposing medieval order…former head of the Congregation for the Doctrine of the Faith…snuffing out reform and reformers… the arch enemy of modernity, canceller of Christmas Parties and Papal rock concerts…no more Bob Dylan in the Vatican, no more Dionne Warwick, no more Whitney Houston. No more fun.

They eat some more.

POPE BENEDICT: Very good.

But then he freezes, and looks into the distance – deep in thought. She finally notices.

SISTER BRIGITTA: Your holiness? If there is anything you would like to discuss…

BENEDICT looks back at her, eats a few more mouthfuls of soup. SISTER BRIGITTA does the same until she notices that BENEDICT is not moving.

SISTER BRIGITTA: Your holiness?

POPE BENEDICT: I am thinking of abdicating.

SISTER BRIGITTA: Abdicating?

POPE BENEDICT: Retiring. Resigning the papacy.

SISTER BRIGITTA: I don't understand.

POPE BENEDICT: I wish that you should know. That I am considering it.

SISTER BRIGITTA: Considering what?

POPE BENEDICT: Resigning. As Pope. Standing down.

SISTER BRIGITTA: You are joking. Your holiness. Resigning?

SISTER BRIGITTA Claps her hands over her cheeks in shock –

SISTER BRIGITTA: Kann nicht wahr sein. But…but…your holiness…it can't…can't be true.

POPE BENEDICT: There have been abdications before. Not for 700 years, I grant you.

SISTER BRIGITTA: But…you are the Pope…

POPE BENEDICT: Yes. I am.

SISTER BRIGITTA: Holy father…

SISTER BRIGITTA Makes another SIGN OF THE CROSS and begins to cry.

The POPE eats another couple of mouthfuls of soup. SISTER BRIGITTA stares at him then at her plate.

POPE BENEDICT: Come now. Eat your soup.

(Eats a spoonful, then.)

Are you crying? Come.

SISTER BRIGITTA: Forgive me.

The pontiff passes her a handkerchief. She wipes her eyes.

POPE BENEDICT: Perhaps…I should not have told you. Such news is too heavy. It was selfish of me.

SISTER BRIGITTA: It is…it is not possible.

POPE BENEDICT: Believe me…I am aware of the shock-waves… of the ramifications… They are deep…they are wide. Who should know better than I?

(Pause.)

Be at peace, sister…be at peace.

The POPE then rises from the table –

POPE BENEDICT: Let us thank the Lord again for the excellent German food we have received.

A rumble of thunder and he walks across the room, listening intently to the rain on the rooftops as it intensifies…

SISTER BRIGITTA watches him, a man in turmoil…

POPE BENEDICT: The early popes, for three centuries, were martyrs. And Rome? Rome was the capital and headquarters for persecution. The history of the papacy is rooted in suffering. I know.

(Beat.)

On my 78th birthday, still just a cardinal, but due for retirement, I gave a little speech to my co-workers. Before I blew out the candles – so many candles!–I said I was looking forward to a time of peace and tranquility. I understated it. I ached for retirement. To go back to Bavaria. To live again in my little village of Pentling, with Georg my brother, in a small house, with my cats, my books, my piano, my Mozart…enjoy what remains of my life.

(Beat.)

Three days later I was Pope. Pope.

Pope.

POPE!

Pope.

SISTER BRIGITTA: Pope.

27

POPE BENEDICT: God's Bishop. Christ's Vicar in the Chair Of St Peter! Head of the Holy See and the Universal Church and *1.2 billion souls*!

265th pope *at the age of 78! Who gets a new job at 78?!* The age of Ronald Reagan when he retired – this is the closest comparison – and Reagan could no longer tie his shoes at the end!

SISTER BRIGITTA: Thank God you were chosen.

POPE BENEDICT: You can't imagine the shock – to be told you have been chosen…when all you planned to do was…eat Knoedel…and allow yourself a small glass…just a small glass of Weisbier.

SISTER BRIGITTA: You were the overwhelming choice!

POPE BENEDICT: Not so. Not so. Not at all. It took two days… four ballots…The cardinals of the conclave…very solemn… one by one going up to put their votes in the urn and looking up at the Last Judgement by Michelangelo. Tension was high. A choice was not obvious. I was on the edge of my chair, wringing my hands, I could hardly breath…thinking praying…not me, Lord not me. Of course, as John Paul's advisor I was an easy option for them. So the debate soon became…"If not Ratzinger then who?" "If not Razinger then who?" And there was one…one was about to overtake me… one who, on the last ballot, threw his supporters behind me…

SISTER BRIGITTA: Who?

POPE BENEDICT: He consigned me…to this calvary. And then they told me. You know how they tell you you have won? "Won"! You must not speak of this – I will confess to you, my TV friend…my Bavarian cultural attache…

SISTER BRIGITTA blushes and lowers her head, smiling –

POPE BENEDICT: They burned the ballots, named me Pope, but the smoke…would not rise, it leaked from the furnace, filled the Sala Regia. I was pope. Habeas Papam. But all I could think was, unless someone opens a door quickly the entire church leadership will be wiped out.

He returns to the table and SISTER BRIGITTA Rises to replenish his bowl.

POPE BENEDICT: Another Knoedel perhaps. No half. Half.

SISTER BRIGITTA: Your holiness. You are tired, that is all. You need rest. A week with no duties, in Castel Gandolfo.

POPE BENEDICT: Sister, it is more serious than that. Every day the crisis worsens. And there are other things, I cannot speak of. I am insufficient to the task, and the task is great! The choice of me was a mistake.

SISTER BRIGITTA: No, please do not say such a thing. Forgive me, but your holiness has been a perfect servant…

POPE BENEDICT: A safe option, that's why I was on the ballot. Someone safe. After John Paul's theatrics, his outreach, his travel, travel, travel – Was there a run-way anywhere in the world left unkissed by that man? – mother church needed to rest and do some house-keeping. *That* was why I was chosen, house-keeper *nummer eins…putz-frau* in chief! Someone steady, to re-assert, protect and strengthen ancient doctrine. In short, to make sure overdue reforms *remained* overdue. But people's souls ache for certainty. *Unchanging truths*. You're right…a little more salt.

He only notices now that SISTER BRIGITTA is sitting in shock, grievously worried.

POPE BENEDICT: I'm sorry. I have upset you. I should not have burdened you. But I need to share these thoughts with someone.

SISTER BRIGITTA: Your holiness? No-one else…knows? No-one else knows of this?

POPE BENEDICT: No. You're the first.

SISTER BRIGITTA: But your mind is not made up? Your holiness?

The POPE salts his soup and leaves the question hanging…

SISTER BRIGITTA: May I…may I speak…on this subject?

POPE BENEDICT: May you? Yes. I am interested in your thoughts. You have also given your whole life to your faith. You have a right to make your case. My decision is your decision.

SISTER BRIGITTA: Then your holiness…I pray you, think again.

POPE BENEDICT: Speak. Speak. It will not hurt me to hear another view.

SISTER BRIGITTA: You cannot resign.

POPE BENEDICT: Cannot you say?

SISTER BRIGITTA: Forgive me, but…no. You cannot. It is impossible.

POPE BENEDICT: Impossible?!

SISTER BRIGITTA: Quite impossible. You have been chosen to be Pope…spiritual president of the World! You…you…

SISTER BRIGITTA has begun to cry again. She uses the POPE's handkerchief. She kneels.

SISTER BRIGITTA: Forgive me, your holiness, but…Forgive me.

POPE BENEDICT: Hush. Hush. Sister. Rise. Rise. Dry your eyes. I'm here to watch TV. Come back to the table. It is you who must forgive me. I should never have burdened you with such a monolithic matter. It was wrong to confide my doubts to you.

SISTER BRIGITTA: Only doubts? You mind is not made up?

POPE BENEDICT: Not...entirely.

SISTER BRIGITTA: Thank God.

POPE BENEDICT: And I thank you for giving me a foretaste of what's to come. *Should* I abdicate I will be caste as a failure. Or a traitor. " "The Rotweiller lost his teeth!" He ruined the tradition he was chosen to defend.

SISTER BRIGITTA: I was not saying...

POPE BENEDICT: You don't have to. I know it already. A traditionalist does not break with a seven hundred year old tradition...unless...

POPE BENEDICT cannot finish the thought...or does not want to...

SISTER BRIGITTA: Unless?

POPE BENEDICT: How long do we have? Before our program starts?

SISTER BRIGITTA: Oh. I...I need to tune the...the aerial...

POPE BENEDICT: Will it take long?

SISTER BRIGITTA: The signal...

POPE BENEDICT: Strange how some days it's good, some days it's bad.

SISTER BRIGITTA: A mystery.

POPE BENEDICT: *(Watching her.)* I hate to miss the beginning. If you don't know who the corpse is it's no fun at all learning who is the culprit.

SISTER BRIGITTA Goes to the TV set. Turns it on, begins to tune the set…

POPE BENEDICT: Our poor little Rex. In the hands of those monsters.

SISTER BRIGITTA: I had it earlier…and then I lost it…just…

POPE BENEDICT: There it is! You had it!

SISTER BRIGITTA: Did I?

POPE BENEDICT: Yes, yes. But it's gone again now. Shall I open the window? Would that – ?

SISTER BRIGITTA: No. It makes no difference. The signal is coming all the way from Austria. It won't stop at the windowsill.

POPE BENEDICT: *(Annoyed.)* Rome is full of TV's, sister. If you had just told me you had a problem with this *(TV)* –

On her knees before the TV, she breaks down, cries again.

Not good at dealing with high emotion, he makes a sacrifice, and turns the TV off, and walks away from her, to look out at the storm.

Finally…

SISTER BRIGITTA: You have left me troubled. I will not sleep now. For worrying. May I ask…why? Why you chose me? Chose to tell me?

POPE BENEDICT: Who else should I tell? I have no friends, sister. I have my brother, but I dare not discuss it with him. I know his arguments already.

And my assistants, my juniors…out of the question. And I feel at peace here, in your lovely apartment, I suppose. I feel at home.

SISTER BRIGITTA: But I cannot advise you.

POPE BENEDICT: Good! *Because* you cannot advise me I chose you. I do not seek advice. This thing…if I am to do it…will tear the church in two. But I am no longer strong enough, in body or mind. And when the Pope is no longer able to fulfill his duties then it is his duty to resign.

SISTER BRIGITTA nods, as she walks away from him.

POPE BENEDICT: You are nodding. Don't just nod! Where are you going? Tell me what you think! I will not bite. We are old friends.

SISTER BRIGITTA: Pope John Paul II –

POPE BENEDICT: Yes! Yes, yes, I know…Paul John Paul II… yes…he would not have dreamt of abdicating.

SISTER BRIGITTA: He was in a wheelchair! Incapacitated for years with Parkinsons, unable to dress himself, unable to speak!

(Beat.)

Are you under pressure to resign?

Silence…

SISTER BRIGITTA *(CONT'D.)*: It just does not sound like a decision you would make. Is there something…?

Silence…BENEDICT sits in a chair, troubled.

SISTER BRIGITTA *(CONT'D.)*: I will make coffee. I have your favorite blend – I went down into the Campo DiFiori – Columbia Luminosa.

POPE BENEDICT: Even the name revives!

(Beat.)

Saint Clement 1…Pontian…Silverio…Benedict IX…
Gregory VI…and Celestine V. There are precedents for
resignation. Celestine lasted only four months as Pope.

SISTER BRIGITTA: In what year?

POPE BENEDICT: 1295.

SISTER BRIGITTA: 719 years ago.

POPE BENEDICT: Mmmm.

SISTER BRIGITTA: Are you in poor health?

POPE BENEDICT: For my age, not so poor. My feet are swollen.
From travel. Ceremonies.

SISTER BRIGITTA goes to him and begins to loosen his shoes…

POPE BENEDICT: It's…please…I didn't…

SISTER BRIGITTA: Let me loosen your shoes.

POPE BENEDICT: I am not a natural leader. *You* talk to people.
What do they say of me?

SISTER BRIGITTA: Well…

POPE BENEDICT: Go on.

SISTER BRIGITTA: Some say…you are…

POPE BENEDICT: Please.

SISTER BRIGITTA: …a little cold, sometimes.

POPE BENEDICT: There. And?

SISTER BRIGITTA: And lacking in charisma.

POPE BENEDICT: It's true. I prefer my own company. My natural
urge is to withdraw.

SISTER BRIGITTA: "A hermit crab, dreaming of his shell."

POPE BENEDICT: I see. Well, I suppose –

SISTER BRIGITTA: *(Interrupting him, warming to the challenge.)* – and that, after seven years, the church needs someone with more talent, less *shell* – someone younger, vigorous, charismatic...someone who can deal with condoms.

POPE BENEDICT: Condoms?

SISTER BRIGITTA: Should they or should they not be permitted in Africa to prevent the spread of HIV? Condoms, divorce, should the church adapt and sanction divorce?

POPE BENEDICT: I –

SISTER BRIGITTA: Homosexual Priests?

POPE BENEDICT: Sister –

SISTER BRIGITTA: A woman who has had an abortion, can she be allowed by her local priest to receive the sacraments?

POPE BENEDICT: The sac –

SISTER BRIGITTA: Women priests? Then there is money laundering in the Vatican Bank.

POPE BENEDICT: So many problems.

SISTER BRIGITTA: And the Vatileaks Scandal. Your own butler stealing your personal papers and giving them to the press!

POPE BENEDICT: Mmm, yes, yes.

SISTER BRIGITTA: And then there is Islam – Holy Father.

POPE BENEDICT: Islam.

SISTER BRIGITTA.: Islam. The rise of Islam.

POPE BENEDICT: *(Erupting.)* I spoke from my heart about Islam!

Distant THUNDER.

SISTER BRIGITTA: – and upset the entire Muslim world!

POPE BENEDICT: I was misunderstood!

SISTER BRIGITTA: Not to mention the Curia.

POPE BENEDICT: No pope has ever –

POPE BENEDICT: Pray for me… pray for me…

SISTER BRIGITTA: You have failed to reform the Curia, which is full of infighting and blackmail. The gay lobby inside the Vatican, with long-held control.

SISTER BRIGITTA: And then the Gotti Tedeschi affair!

POPE BENEDICT: Ohhhhhhhhh!

SISTER BRIGITTA: And worst of all, the evil matter of sex abuse, of filthy priests.

POPE BENEDICT: SISTER! PEACE!

Big roll of THUNDER. He silences her and she realises she has spoken truth to power and gone far too far. Silence, then –

POPE BENEDICT: And yet – clearly lacking the strength and talent to resolve all these matters, you say I must not resign?

She gathers her arguments afresh –

SISTER BRIGITTA: You must protect the Christian model of total sacrifice. To resign the Petrine Ministry, your Holiness, is to depart from the example of Jesus who gave his life for the salvation of mankind.

POPE BENEDICT: So, the chair of St Peter must be my cross?

SISTER BRIGITTA: Christ established it so. And his crown one of thorns.

POPE BENEDICT: Sister, you are a biblical scholar…who has relieved my feet but intensified my suffering.

SISTER BRIGITTA: I mean only to remind you of what you know already.

POPE BENEDICT: I do not forget. I wish I could do so. But my memory, my mind, still functions.

SISTER BRIGITTA: Then what need to resign? We do not need an athlete. We need wisdom. *(His laces are loosened.)* There!

POPE BENEDICT: Thank you. And now, no more heavy talk. It is time for our program.

SISTER BRIGITTA: I cannot watch the program now. I am too upset.

POPE BENEDICT: It will do you good. Calm you. Clear your mind. I beg you, see if you can get a good picture with this bad weather…

SISTER BRIGITTA reluctantly starts tuning the set…staring at him.

POPE BENEDICT *(CONT'D.)*: I have never said No to God. Never. If my thinking is wrong then it his duty to change my mind. His! *He* must instruct *me*. And he has always spoken to me. Told me what to do. I wait on his word.

SISTER BRIGITTA makes the sign of the cross.

SISTER BRIGITTA: But who could possibly replace you? At such a time of crisis?

POPE BENEDICT: There is one. There is one I am thinking about. One who could do it. Perhaps. One name that God has put into my mind. But…he is not a perfect choice. He speaks off-the-cuff. *Spontaneous!* I sense there is ego there. Opinions. He represents 'change'. Well, perhaps *he* could change. Perhaps God could change *him*?

SISTER BRIGITTA: Cardinal…

POPE BENEDICT: Bergoglio. The Argentinian. A man of great spirit.

SISTER BRIGITTA: Your rival.

POPE BENEDICT: I have no rivals.

The Pope points at the TV set…SISTER BRIGITTA has managed to find the picture.

POPE BENEDICT *(CONT'D.)*: There! *(Picture goes but then comes back.)* Oh, almost. Almost. Slower…slower! Oh it's gone again. Is there no other TV? Something more modern? It looks very old.

SISTER BRIGITTA: We can't afford to change it. And we have our vow of poverty.

POPE BENEDICT: I will speak to Archbishop Ganswein. We will put it on the Vatican budget. A nice new –

(Suddenly.)

Ah! There! You have it! That's it. You have it. Don't touch it!

SISTER BRIGITTA: It's…it's a poor picture.

POPE BENEDICT: The world is in tumult. Where shall I sit?

SISTER BRIGITTA: In your chair. In your normal chair, Holy Father.

POPE BENEDICT: Do we…do we have any sound?

SISTER BRIGITTA: I don't know. Um. Yes. It's on mute…while the commercials are on.

POPE BENEDICT: Good. But let's turn it up, sister, when the theme song begins. To get us in the mood. Please don't worry.

SISTER M.: Oh, your coffee!   POPE BENEDICT *(CONT'D.)*:
Your coffee…   I don't need coffee.

SISTER BRIGITTA brings the coffee to POPE BENEDICT.

POPE BENEDICT *(CONT'D.)*: Danke.

SISTER BRIGITTA: Forgive me. It is such a terrible shock. Most shocking day of my life. A calamity for the whole world.

SISTER BRIGITTA sits. He tries to calm her…

POPE BENEDICT: Sshhhh. Ah sister. Ssshhh now. Why should life be so difficult? So full of pain? So mysterious? Peace now. I have not made up my mind. Don't despair. You have made good and powerful arguments. I will reflect on them. Thank you sister.

(To the TV.)

Oh! Here it is! Sound! Sound!

SISTER BRIGITTA points the remote control, but the sound does not come on.

POPE BENEDICT *(CONT'D.)*: Sound, sound, sound!

SISTER BRIGITTA: Forgive me. I'm…it…

POPE BENEDICT: Can we…is there something…?

SISTER BRIGITTA crosses to the TV set and turns up the volume manually. The nervous tension is high as they wait to find out if Rex is dead or alive…

POPE BENEDICT *(CONT'D.)*: Ah! Serh gut. Serrrhhh gut…

SISTER BRIGITTA: Bitte schön. Bitte schön…

POPE BENEDICT: All the way from Austria…

SISTER BRIGITTA: Austria…yes…then…deep space…then here…

POPE BENEDICT: *(Nervous.)* Oh dear God.

They both make the SIGN OF THE CROSS and cannot bear the tension as they watch the opening credits…

The POPE blindly reaches out his hand to the NUN and she does the same. They hold hands as the program starts – and then they see – that REX is alive!

POPE BENEDICT *(CONT'D.)*: He's alive! Sister? Look, he's alive! Oh thank God! He's come back to us! Our little dog…has come back to us!

The POPE springs to his feet and the NUN and they hug in relief.

SCENE 2

A SPOT LIGHT rises. Into the pool of divine light comes CARDINAL JORGE BERGOGLIO, the Argentinian. He delivers his sermon to the congregation…

CARDINAL BERGOGLIO: I used to have a TV. I like to watch football.

(Beat.)

My team is…well, I can tell anyone who is interested later.

(Beat.)

A TV it needs…an aerial. And a signal. Some days the signal is bad-- who knows why, it's just bad. Like prayer. Some days the signal from God is strong, it goes very well, you feel that connection, really plugged in, in direct communication, but other days…it's all you can do to feel "well, I tried…at least today I tried."

(Beat.)

I am a sinner. This is the most accurate definition. It is not a figure of speech, a literary trope. I am a sinner. Seventy-five years ago, a young woman, Regina María Bergoglio, my mother, gave birth to the sinner you see before you. Since the age of reason the irony is that I have always tried to do the right thing, to keep my silly ears open so I could hear His voice. But I too often failed. And in my failure, others suffered. *You* suffered. And now, brothers and sisters…my time is up. My ministry is at an end. So I come to the barios of Bueos Aires…to this little makeshift house of worship this morning to bid you goodbye. To thank you for all you have given me, and to ask your forgiveness for any pain or loss of faith you have suffered as a result of me or my actions. A priest is a flawed vessel. Make your own connections to God. Stay connected. Go in peace to love and serve the Lord.

Lights up on SCENE TWO. A small altar in a shanty hut in a slum (Villa 31) in Buenos Aires. This is the "VILLA MISERIA" – the area of the city inhabited by BEGGARS, CRIMINALS, DRUG DEALERS.

After BERGOGLIO removes his priestly vestments, he packs up his portable altar…wraps the cheap CRUCIFIX in a cloth, and then blows out the single candle and puts it back into his bag. During this he hums a slow tune…we cannot at first recognise it.

Enter, unseen, SISTER SOPHIA, a 30 year old super-idealistic Nun. She smiles.

SISTER SOPHIA: Eminence?

CARDINAL BERGOGLIO: Ah! Sister!

SISTER SOPHIA: What hymn is that? Something – ?

CARDINAL BERGOGLIO: ABBA. 'Dancing Queen'. ABBA.

He starts singing 'Dancing Queen'.

As she starts to laugh, he takes her and begins to tango with her!

SISTER SOPHIA: Oh no! Ha! Ha!

He continues singing until the chorus.

They stop, laughing.

SISTER SOPHIA: Anybody could be that guy...

CARDINAL BERGOGLIO: Anybody...could be that guy.

The CARDINAL returns to his task.

SISTER SOPHIA: Let me help you.

The SISTER begins to help him pack up the altar.

CARDINAL BERGOGLIO: Did you ever have a boyfriend, sister? Ever?

SISTER SOPHIA: No! Heavens no. No. No, no, no.

CARDINAL BERGOGLIO: No?

SISTER SOPHIA: No!

CARDINAL BERGOGLIO: No experience of romance?

SISTER SOPHIA: Ummm...no.

CARDINAL BERGOGLIO: You were young when you came to convent life.

SISTER SOPHIA: Si. At twelve I came to the convent. My family was poor, could not provide for me.

CARDINAL BERGOGLIO: Twelve?! So young!

SISTER SOPHIA: My grandparents dropped me off at the convent gate.

CARDINAL BERGOGLIO: Ha! But you had a sense of vocation even then? No?

SISTER SOPHIA: At twelve, what does it matter what you think? I remember I was afraid. The boarding school was cold and alien. I missed my family. But the sisters were good to me. And there was a surprising amount of laughter. Nuns laugh a lot.

CARDINAL BERGOGLIO: And then? Something happened? Something made you want to be a nun.

SISTER SOPHIA: Si.

CARDINAL BERGOGLIO: And what was it?

SISTER SOPHIA: You.

CARDINAL BERGOGLIO: Me? No. Me? No.

SISTER SOPHIA: Si. You, father. You. I heard you speak. Give one of your sermons, about how the church must listen to, answer, and free the poor.

CARDINAL BERGOGLIO: And?

SISTER SOPHIA: You quoted the psalms. "This poor man cried, and the Lord heard him." And I decided, right then, to place my life, as you had, in the service of the poor. To give up family, the normal life, for others.

CARDINAL BERGOGLIO: Oh child –

SISTER SOPHIA: Solidarity, amongst all humanity, making sure none is left behind. I want a new kind of world. With different rules.

CARDINAL BERGOGLIO: Indeed.

SISTER SOPHIA: And this work, the fine and holy work, necessary work, it has hardly begun.

CARDINAL BERGOGLIO: Si.

SISTER SOPHIA: Which is why, father, why you must not resign.

CARDINAL BERGOGLIO: Ah! Now I see what you are up to.

(Correcting her.)

But not "resign" – retire. I am old.

SISTER SOPHIA: You cannot. You, *your voice*, is needed. There is an opportunity now, with technology, with the right person, the right message, to bring people together in great numbers.

CARDINAL BERGOGLIO: Sister, I am sorry. It is already decided. Help me now. Help me clear up.

In silence they clear up, until –

SISTER SOPHIA: If I may ask, do you remember the moment you were called, your Eminence? By God?

CARDINAL BERGOGLIO: I do. I do indeed. Si.

SISTER SOPHIA: You heard his voice?

CARDINAL BERGOGLIO: I knew our local priest very well…he used to rely on me to tell him jokes. He would see me on the street and call out: "Jorge Bergoglio! Come and tell me a joke." He liked dirty jokes. I was a bouncer in a tango club so I got to hear plenty! Ha!Ha!

SISTER SOPHIA: A bouncer?

CARDINAL BERGOGLIO: Si! So I would say: "Father, I have one." And he would say "Go on my son" and I would tell him one, like, like, like, ha!…Ha!Ha!Ha!… "Two men are searching for their wives in a large supermarket. They decide to team up. The first man asks the second:

"So what does your wife look like?"

"Okay, well, she's about six foot tall, long legs, mini skirt, and blonde. How about yours?" The first man ponders and then replies: "Ah, let's just look for yours." Ha!Ha!Ha!

SISTER SOPHIA: On no.

CARDINAL BERGOGLIO: He would laugh as he walked away and call back: "*Straight to confession, Bergoglio! Straight to confession!*" And it was in confession, one day, that I received my call. Something made me go in to the Basilica this day, I don't know what, but a force drew me there, and the church was empty but the red light, on the confession box, told me the priest was hearing confession, so I went in, and the priest was a stranger. I asked him where he was from and said, from the priest's Home for the Sick.

SISTER SOPHIA: He was ill?

CARDINAL BERGOGLIO: Cancer, he told me. Leukemia. So I asked him why he was here now, and he told me he awoke that morning at 6 am and the Lord had told him to get out of his sick bed and come to the Basilica to hear confession. And until I came, he had seen no-one, no-one else had shown up, so he suspected that the Lord had intended that he be there for me. Just for me. And I don't know what I confessed to him, but when I left that little box, it was very strange…a feeling of grace came over me and I knew…I just knew… and my path was set…my course clear.

SISTER SOPHIA: Your Eminence…

CARDINAL BERGOGLIO: What is it, sister?

SISTER SOPHIA: Would you…hear my confession?

CARDINAL BERGOGLIO: Your confession?

SISTER SOPHIA: Si.

CARDINAL BERGOGLIO: Of course. Of course. But let me finish packing up first.

(As they clear up.)

So it is your confession that brings you down here, to the barrios, to the slums of Buenos Aires? Could you not find a priest closer to home?

SISTER SOPHIA: I was told I would find you here, your Eminence, serving the poor this morning. Ministering mass. The local people must have been shocked to see you. A Cardinal in their midst!

CARDINAL BERGOGLIO: Yes, an apparition. We had a good crowd. Better than the Basilica. And they were all ears. Hungry. Thirsting. This is where I should have based my work, sister…instead of being a bureaucrat, in high office, losing my way, my sense of vocation in decision-making and rubber stamps and envelopes and photocopies and paper work and emails. No, I came down here this morning to bid this place goodbye, the simple people goodbye. This is where Fathers Yorio and Jalics based their radical ministry. The very ministry I opposed when I was head of the Jesuits, the ministry I shut down. They were right, and I was wrong. Their response was the correct one. In the face of evil you must resist, with everything you have.

(Beat.)

You are too young to remember those dark times.

SISTER SOPHIA: Si.

CARDINAL BERGOGLIO: Then you are lucky.

SISTER SOPHIA: Not so lucky. Not lucky.

CARDINAL BERGOGLIO: Sister? Oh. I see. I'm sorry.

SISTER SOPHIA: Both my parents…they were among the last to vanish.

CARDINAL BERGOGLIO: Both?

SISTER SOPHIA: I was…I was only six months old. My father was taken first. They came to the house. Later they found his body in a pit. Shot many times. Military machine gun. He made suits. He was a tailor. The most wonderful suits. The best cloth. The finest detail. The shot him in one of his beautiful suits. My mother, soon after, she was taken, never found. She liked to sing. I like to think I can remember the sound of her voice. My grandparents raised me after that.

CARDINAL BERGOGLIO: Oh dear child. May Jesus give you comfort and peace.

SISTER SOPHIA: He does. He does, father. But I still feel great anger. At the injustice. At the monsters, those monsters, those Generals and Admirals, those men, who killed their own brothers and sisters, mothers and children, in their tens of thousands…and I am angry still at all those who stood by and did nothing to stop it, all those who remained silent just to stay out of trouble.

BERGOGLIO stares at her –

SISTER SOPHIA: That is why I believe in your mission so much. Why you are needed. You are the voice of resistance. Of saying No to power. Of resistance! Standing up to the brutes, and injustice, and evil, no matter the cost.

(Beat.)

Did you also lose people close to you? Family?

At first BERGOGLIO cannot reply – so challenged is he by her words.

SISTER SOPHIA: I'm sorry.

CARDINAL BERGOGLIO: Not family. *(Beat.)* My dear friend, Esther, Esther Ballestrino – she taught me chemistry, gave me forbidden copies of Karl Marx, Das Kapital, and Liberation Theology – they seized lovely Esther from these very slums where she was also working with the poor.

SISTER SOPHIA: And what did they do to her?

CARDINAL BERGOGLIO: Be at peace sister.

SISTER SOPHIA: Please father. Tell me. What did they do to her? I have heard every story. What did they do to Esther, your friend?

CARDINAL BERGOGLIO: They put a bag over her head, bound her hands and feet, drugged her, then flew her out over the ocean in an army helicopter, and rolled her body out the back door where it fell, fell, down, down…into the ocean.

SISTER SOPHIA makes the sign of the cross.

SISTER SOPHIA: Dear God.

CARDINAL BERGOGLIO: Too many funerals were conducted here…just a few of the tens of thousands murdered whose only crime was to speak – with the voice of truth, of opposition, liberation, and of love – to tyrants with guns. Sister, you are a long way from home this morning?

SISTER SOPHIA: I came to find you. When I heard the rumors of your resignation. To beg you to think again.

CARDINAL BERGOGLIO: I am 75. I have reached the official age of retirement for priests. No one should be surprised.

SISTER SOPHIA: Why are you leaving? You have your health. It cannot be your age. You have other reasons?

He doesn't reply but clearly he does –

SISTER SOPHIA: What other reasons?

CARDINAL BERGOGLIO: They are for me and God.

SISTER SOPHIA: Whatever the reasons I pray you think again.

CARDINAL BERGOGLIO: You must be giving your superiors a great headache.

SISTER SOPHIA: To retire at 75 may be normal for others, but not for you, your eminence. We need you too much.

CARDINAL BERGOGLIO: Ah, there is nothing special about me except my limitations.

SISTER SOPHIA: But there is! There is! We *need* you. The church of Argentina needs you. And the Pope needs you.

CARDINAL BERGOGLIO: The Pope? Ha! Benedict will be the first to wish to see the back of me, believe me. We have our differences.

They begin now to fold up the altar cloth, together.

CARDINAL BERGOGLIO: Good sister, let me ask you a question…a general question. What would you do if you'd written *twice* to someone, made your intentions very clear, and that person did not write back?

SISTER SOPHIA: I would assume…the person is angry…or busy. Who is the person?

CARDINAL BERGOGLIO: The Pope.

SISTER SOPHIA: *Busy.*

CARDINAL BERGOGLIO: I simply need his signature – on my resignation papers. Do I write again?

SISTER SOPHIA: Two cats.

(Pause.)

He has two cats…

CARDINAL BERGOGLIO: Yes, and 1.2 billion followers. Perhaps I must go to him.

SISTER SOPHIA: To Rome?

CARDINAL BERGOGLIO: I doubt he will come here, to the Villa Miseria, to the little tin palaces of the doomed. His red slippers might get dirty.

SISTER SOPHIA: How can you retire--so many need you, love you? Perhaps the Pope sees this also--sees how you are still needed here.

CARDINAL BERGOGLIO: How should he see it, from his castle? These would be impressive binoculars. I should go to him. You know, that's what I should do. Go to *him!* Insist that he sign my resignation papers.

SISTER SOPHIA: Is it true, you came second in the voting for the last papal conclave?

CARDINAL BERGOGLIO: Well…it's not like the world cup. And how did you hear this? Gossip is work for idle hands.

SISTER SOPHIA: But you threw your votes in behind him?

CARDINAL BERGOGLIO: Worse and worse! I did not want to be a figure of division. God's will is not divisive. It is unifying. And I'm a Jesuit. We are prohibited from seeking high office. There has never been a Jesuit Pope.

SISTER SOPHIA: And yet, you came second.

CARDINAL BERGOGLIO: It's true. In the end if was just Cardinal Josef Ratzinger and myself. Facing each other. A penalty shoot out.

(Mimes kicking the goal.)

You might say I chose not to defend my goal. And I was relieved. You can't imagine…

I was even there, when they dressed him, in his robes of office, when they slid the Ring Of The Fisherman on his finger, in the anteroom to the balcony over St Peters Square, the room they call "La Stanza Delle Lacrime"…

The Room Of Tears, where so many popes have wept in the moment where the burden of office is laid upon them. Such relief I felt, that I…I could just go home, to Buenos Aires, and count the days until my retirement. And now the day is here. I am 75, and just one signature away from freedom!

SISTER SOPHIA: I hope the Pope is too busy to write.

CARDINAL BERGOGLIO: Si. He is very busy. Shutting out the winds of change must take great effort. Snuffing out…

(Snuffs out with his fingers a candle.)

…every new flame. Silencing every new voice. He is the prince of the status quo and in these times, when all is flux, he must be the busiest man alive.

SISTER SOPHIA: It is not too late to hope for change, if we are prepared to keep working for it.

CARDINAL BERGOGLIO: Under this pope? Hopeless. For the last ten years I have been calling on the church to change, to speak for the millions crying out for it. God is not afraid of new things. Why can we not sail from our safe harbour into the deep of the contemporary world?

They have finished clearing up the altar.

CARDINAL BERGOGLIO: Come sister. Kneel. Let me hear your confession. Then I will go and book my flight to Rome.

The sister kneels behind a chair upon which BERGOGLIO sits. BERGOGLIO closes his eyes…

CARDINAL BERGOGLIO: When you are ready, sister. May the Lord be in your heart and help you to confess your sins with true sorrow.

SISTER SOPHIA: *(Makes Sign Of The Cross.)* Bless me father for I have sinned. It has been six days since my last confession.

CARDINAL BERGOGLIO: And how have you sinned, sister? Make a full and frank confession to me now…God is listening. You are alone with God.

SISTER SOPHIA: My sin is a selfish one. I have been praying… praying…that the rumors are not true and that Cardinal Bergoglio will not resign. That is my sin. For the sake of the church I have been selfishly praying that he will not leave us at a time when our need for him, for someone like him, has never been greater.

CARDINAL BERGOGLIO: That is your sin?

SISTER SOPHIA: Si, father.

Silence…

CARDINAL BERGOGLIO: Jesus came and stood in their midst and he breathed upon them, and said unto them, 'Receive the Holy Spirit…whose sins you shall forgive, they are forgiven them…and whose sins you shall retain, they are retained… they are retained…'

(With a sigh, quickly wrapping it up.)

For your penance, say three Hail Mary's and two Our Father's and try to sin no more. Go in peace to love and serve the Lord, in the name of the Father and the Son and the Holy Ghost amen.

SISTER SOPHIA: Amen.

BERGOGLIO arises quickly, as if in a hurry now.

SISTER SOPHIA: Thank you Your Eminence.

She watches him, sees she has upset him.

CARDINAL BERGOGLIO: Was there something else?

SISTER SOPHIA: No.

CARDINAL BERGOGLIO: What more can I give? I am empty. An empty vessel.

SISTER SOPHIA: If you would only say that you would think about it.

CARDINAL BERGOGLIO: Think about it?

SISTER SOPHIA: Think *again*...about the possibility of a few more years. Even if you give us two or three. Then I could breathe more freely again.

He shakes his head, in admiration of her –

CARDINAL BERGOGLIO: Sister, what should happen is I resign and *you* should take over! You are a *very* persuasive person. I will not change my mind but I will think on what you have said today. But that is all.

SISTER SOPHIA: I speak for the entire church of Argentina!

CARDINAL BERGOGLIO: Now if I could be alone.

SISTER SOPHIA: *(Happier now.)* Si. Si. Bless you, bless you.

CARDINAL BERGOGLIO: Bless you. And be careful on your journey out of the slums. It is full of beggars and bandits, who are not all friends of the clergy.

SISTER SOPHIA suddenly kisses BERGOGLIO's hand...then exits, happily.

BERGOGLIO is alone. He gathers his things. And then his MOBILE PHONE rings, with its TANGO RING-TONE.

CARDINAL BERGOGLIO: Ah. Gabriel! What is it? Rome? The Vatican? Open it, open it.

(Sings.)

Friday night and the lights are low, looking out for a place to go...

Yes. Yes. His holiness wishes me to…to visit him at his summer residence? Castel Gandolfo? Visit him in Castel Gandolfo…Why?

"Certain matters." Discuss certain matters? Ha! Prayer at work. So, I've been called…to be relieved of my burden at last. We *are* in God's hands, Gabriel! Thank God! We are in his hands! Isn't that remarkable? Ha! I am free. I am to be set free. Adios.

BERGOGLIO hangs up.

CARDINAL BERGOGLIO: *(Sings to himself.)* Where they play the right music/ getting in the swing/ You come in to look for a king/ Anybody could be that guy…

(Taking a last look around.)

Free!

BERGOGLIO exits.

ACT 2

SCENE 1

Garden. Castel Gandolfo, the Pope's Summer Residence. August, 2012. A beautiful day. Bird-song.

SISTER BRIGITTA leads CARDINAL (Jorge Mario) BERGOGLIO (76) into the garden, then withdraws.

He is dressed in a cardinal's crimson robes.

He chooses a stone bench upon which to sit.

He waits, looks at his watch.

Enter the POPE's ASSISTANT with a BLACK UMBRELLA for the CARDINAL. The ASSISTANT exits.

The CARDINAL looks up at the sky – will it rain? No. How strange. He sets the umbrella at his side.

He waits.

And then his CELL-PHONE rings. He digs under the layers of FABRIC to try and pull out his phone…he checks the most obvious pockets…but he cannot find the phone.

The CELL-PHONE stops ringing. He sits. He waits. And the CELL-PHONE starts ringing again. He resumes the search…and this time he finds it!

CARDINAL BERGOGLIO: Hola. Oh hola. Sí. Lo siento. Tengo que aprender a poner mi teléfono en vibrar. "Vibrate". No tienes ni idea. ¿Cuántas llamadas echo de menos. Sí. Sí. Eso está bien. Ochoen punto. Sí. Puede confirmar eso. Voy a decir unas palabras. Claro. Sí. Adiós.

Enter POPE BENEDICT (85) in white robes…smiling…He carries a FILE (manila folder).

POPE BENEDICT: Cardinal Bergoglio! Welcome to the gardens of Castel Gandolfo.

CARDINAL BERGOGLIO:	POPE BENEDICT: No, no.
Ultima qua convénimus	No, no.
occasione, latine locuti	
sumus.	

The POPE sets the file on the stone bench as he crosses to the CARDINAL. They grasp each others hands and warmly shake them repeatedly.

CARDINAL BERGOGLIO: Last time we met we spoke Latin.

POPE BENEDICT: *That* was a very short meeting. Conventus brevissimus erat.

CARDINAL BERGOGLIO: But I was never the student you were, Holy Father.

The CARDINAL bends and kisses the POPE's ring…

POPE BENEDICT: Latin is useful, especially when I have to announce bad news to Cardinals. Only twenty percent of them become angry because only twenty percent of them know what I have said! I'm sorry to have kept you waiting. I know you value punctuality.

CARDINAL BERGOGLIO: It's a beautiful afternoon. I have my breviary. I take the last hour as a gift of peace from you. Grazie.

POPE BENEDICT: Paolo, my last assistant – he would have made sure I got here on time. He was perfect.

CARDINAL BERGOGLIO: But now he's in jail.

This earns a sharp look from the POPE.

CARDINAL BERGOGLIO: Would you prefer to walk? We could walk if you preferred.

POPE BENEDICT: That might not be wise…

(Pointing down.)

Your shoelaces are undone.

CARDINAL BERGOGLIO: Oh!

BERGOGLIO hurriedly ties his simple black shoes.

POPE BENEDICT: Your shoes.

CARDINAL BERGOGLIO: Old friends.

POPE BENEDICT: Mmmm.

CARDINAL BERGOGLIO: Are you well, Holy Father?

POPE BENEDICT: At my age better not to ask.

CARDINAL BERGOGLIO: I pray for your strength, in this time of crisis.

POPE BENEDICT: We have weathered many storms. In our 2000 year history we have always been under attack, always remained the unchanging constant, the *Axis Mundi.*

BERGOGLIO, rebuffed, tries to make his point more plainly-

CARDINAL BERGOGLIO: But so many issues *all at once?* Day after day –

POPE BENEDICT: Thank you for coming all this way. Sit. I will stand if you don't mind. This is my hour of exercise. My doctor bought this, this Fitness Watch for me. Don't know what you call it. You see?

Reveals the FITNESS WATCH on his wrist…

POPE BENEDICT: Said "You're in good shape for 86, but very bad shape for a human being." A joke. I think.

BERGOGLIO sits, as the POPE's ASSISTANT arrives with a rolled WHITE UMBRELLA for the POPE, opens it, gives it to the POPE, the withdraws.

POPE BENEDICT: You will be wondering –

(To the ASSISTANT.)

– thank you.

(To BERGOLGIO.)

– why I asked you here.

The heat. Global warming.

BERGOGLIO picks up the BLACK UMBRELLA but does not open it.

CARDINAL BERGOGLIO: Si. Your Holiness, may I ask you straight away, whether you received two letters from me in the last month?

POPE BENEDICT: You wrote to me asking for permission to resign as Cardinal Bishop.

CARDINAL BERGOGLIO: I received no reply. I have my resignation papers with me.

He produces the papers.

POPE BENEDICT: Cardinals are not obliged to offer their resignation when they're seventy five. Are you ill?

CARDINAL BERGOGLIO: I have a problem with my lungs.

POPE BENEDICT: You were born with that. It's not really troubled you since, has it? It's in your file.

CARDINAL BERGOGLIO: My file!?

POPE BENEDICT: We keep files on everyone. You don't have to be flattered. Are you ill? You don't look ill.

CARDINAL BERGOGLIO: I'm not ill.

POPE BENEDICT: In fact you're very active. You walk everywhere. Sometimes use a bicycle.

CARDINAL BERGOGLIO: And I tango once a week.

POPE BENEDICT: You tango? Dance?

CARDINAL BERGOGLIO: I'm Argentinian. Football and tango are compulsory.

(Spinning the closed umbrella, happily.)

POPE BENEDICT: Of course. You dance…with someone?

CARDINAL BERGOGLIO: One might look foolish if one attempted the tango alone. So for the sake of the dignity of my office – yes. *With* someone.

POPE BENEDICT: Retire? Retire--and do what?

CARDINAL BERGOGLIO: Very little.

POPE BENEDICT: Retire, where?

CARDINAL BERGOGLIO: Flores. The Father's House, for retired priests in Flores. The suburb where I was born. My little room is booked, waiting for me.

The nuns will look after me for the few years left to me.
I'm going home.

POPE BENEDICT: Don't mind if I walk about. This thing on my wrist…

He walks…

POPE BENEDICT: …measures my footsteps--counts my daily footsteps. American. 4005…4006…7…and it even tells me off, reprimands me, like a child! Sends me messages… here…here…

He pushes a button on the watch, and we hear: "TIME TO GET MOVING"…

POPE BENEDICT: Ha. Or, or…

He pushes the button again: "WELL DONE! BRAVO! BRAVO!"

POPE BENEDICT: Patronized by a watch! You see?

CARDINAL BERGOGLIO: One does not need a wristwatch if one wants to feel patronized.

The POPE stops and looks at BERGOGLIO as if this is an insult-

POPE BENEDICT: Do you often feel patronized, Cardinal?

CARDINAL BERGOGLIO: At the moment, I feel ignored.

The POPE dismisses his ASSISTANT, takes the UMBRELLA.

POPE BENEDICT: I was always one to follow orders.

Another Papal insult?

POPE BENEDICT: …so – let us obey this American watch.

The POPE collapses the umbrella, begins to pace, checking his fitness watch from time to time. BERGOGLIO remains on the bench.

POPE BENEDICT: We're strangers to each other. We have made so many new Cardinals. The late Pope had a rush of blood…

The watch – says "KEEP MOVING, KEEP MOVING"

POPE BENEDICT: Cardinals, Cardinals, Cardinals…

(Pause.)

You've been one of my harshest critics. There's a lot of competition for that title.

CARDINAL BERGOGLIO: I've never spoken out against you.

POPE BENEDICT: Not directly. When I made it easier to get permission to use the old Tridentine mass, I was criticized because it contains a prayer for the conversion of the Jews.

CARDINAL BERGOGLIO: I never said a word.

POPE BENEDICT: You invited the chief rabbi to a public lunch.

CARDINAL BERGOGLIO: Rabbi Skora and I go back a long way. I made a lot of food. I could not waste it. Wasting food is stealing from the poor.

POPE BENEDICT: You refuse to live in the official Palace of the Archbishop.

CARDINAL BERGOGLIO: It's too grand, it's too big.

POPE BENEDICT: By being so pure and simple you imply that the rest of us are not living simply enough.

CARDINAL BERGOGLIO: Can one ever live simply enough?

POPE BENEDICT: On married priests …

The watch – says "DON'T STOP".

CARDINAL BERGOGLIO: All I said was…I was misquoted. I said celibacy can be a gift. It can also be a curse.

POPE BENEDICT: On homosexuality …

CARDINAL BERGOGLIO: All I said was …

POPE BENEDICT: You were no doubt misquoted again?

CARDINAL BERGOGLIO: Taken out of context.

The POPE stops walking and faces BERGOGLIO.

POPE BENEDICT: Might I suggest you try telling newspapers the opposite of what you think?! Your chances of being quoted correctly might thereby improve!

The watch says: "EXERCISE COMPLETE. WELL DONE" The POPE *is exhausted.*

You openly give the sacraments to those who are out of communion ... to the divorced, for instance ...

BERGOGLIO comes back on this, cutting the POPE off.

CARDINAL BERGOGLIO: I believe giving communion is not a reward for the virtuous. It is food for the starving.

POPE BENEDICT: So what matters is what YOU believe, not what the Church has taught for hundreds of years.

CARDINAL BERGOGLIO: Mark 2.xvii – "I came to call sinners," as the Church has taught for THOUSANDS of years.

POPE BENEDICT: But if we do not draw a line ...

CARDINAL BERGOGLIO: ... or build a wall to separate ...

POPE BENEDICT: You talk about walls as if they're bad things. A house is build of walls. Strong walls.

CARDINAL BERGOGLIO: Did Jesus build walls? His face is the face of Mercy. The bigger the sinner, the warmer the welcome. Mercy is the dynamite that blows down walls.

POPE BENEDICT: You have an answer for everything, don't you? You're clever. You're far too clever. You see my dilemma. You are eloquent. You are popular. If I allow you to resign, it will look like a protest. The Church being attacked from all sides. Why would you want to abandon her to her enemies? Does a shepherd run away when the wolves appear?

CARDINAL BERGOGLIO: I'm not running away. I'll take a parish. I'll be a good shepherd to its people.

POPE BENEDICT: Don't you see? You were very nearly elected Pope. You came second. If you go, that is a criticism. The way you *live* is a criticism. Your SHOES are a criticism.

CARDINAL BERGOGLIO: You don't like my shoes?

POPE BENEDICT: Do not make a joke of everything that I say, please. It's dishonest and cynical. I am the Pope. Have enough respect to show me your real anger.

CARDINAL BERGOGLIO: Holy Father …

POPE BENEDICT: If I allow someone of your standing simply to walk away – it will look like a protest. *Is it a protest? Do you think the Church is failing?*

A GARDENER crosses through the garden, breaking the tension.

POPE BENEDICT: Sit. I need to sit. I'm so tired.

The POPE *sits on the bench. After a pause –*

POPE BENEDICT: *(Softly.)* Do you…think the Church…is failing?

CARDINAL BERGOGLIO: In the west we are losing millions of followers.

POPE BENEDICT: And this is the fault of the Church? It's not the Western permissiveness, this attitude of "anything goes"?

(Beat.)

You said the church was narcissistic. Or is that another misquote?

CARDINAL BERGOGLIO: No. I did say that. It seems to me that your Church –

POPE BENEDICT: My church?

CARDINAL BERGOGLIO: OUR Church…is moving in directions I can't condone … or not moving at all when the times cry out for movement. Holy Father, I no longer wish to be a salesman…

POPE BENEDICT: – a salesman! –

CARDINAL BERGOGLIO: – It's a metaphor. A salesman for a product –

POPE BENEDICT: – a product!

CARDINAL BERGOGLIO: – I *cannot* with *all* conscience endorse. It seems to me that we're no longer part of this world. We don't belong to it. We're not connected.

POPE BENEDICT: "A church that marries the spirit of the age …

CARDINAL BERGOGLIO: … will be widowed in the next age." Yes yes I know.

POPE BENEDICT: *(Anger slowly building.)* When you were leader of the Jesuits in Argentina you had all the books on Marxism removed from the library.

CARDINAL BERGOGLIO: …and I made the seminarians wear cassocks all day – even when they were working in the vegetable garden. And I called civil marriage for homosexuals, the devil's plan.

POPE BENEDICT: You were not unlike me.

CARDINAL BERGOGLIO: I changed.

POPE BENEDICT: No. You compromised.

CARDINAL BERGOGLIO: No. No compromise. I <u>changed</u>. It's a different thing.

POPE BENEDICT: Change is compromise.

CARDINAL BERGOGLIO: Life – the life He gave us – is all change. You are the successor of St. Peter. St. Peter was married!

POPE BENEDICT: Oh, thank you for telling me. I had no idea.

CARDINAL BERGOGLIO: We didn't ask priests to be celibate until 12th Century. Angels! Little mention until the fifth century then suddenly angels are everywhere, like pigeons!

(Beat.)

Divorced people are less virtuous, gay people are wicked, someone who has had an abortion is no longer welcome…

POPE BENEDICT: Enough.

When we require our priests to insist on incredible things, we become incredible. Un-believable.

POPE BENEDICT: Yes. You spoke very candidly in July of last year about your solutions.

CARDINAL BERGOGLIO: I was on holiday.

BENEDICT: Your tongue certainly was. And your solution? Cardinal? Mmm? What was it?

CARDINAL BERGOGLIO: Insist less. Include more. Bring into joyous alignment the beautiful lessons taught in our churches and the beautiful lessons being taught in our schools. The hymn that insists that one plus one equals three will soon lack a choir, no matter how beautiful and ancient the tune.

POPE BENEDICT: You do realise there is a difference between what one thinks and what can be said?

CARDINAL BERGOGLIO: Is there? It's a simple observation: *that nothing is static in nature or in the universe, so why can't God, its maker, change?*

POPE BENEDICT: *(Erupting.)* *No! God does not change!*

CARDINAL BERGOGLIO: If he reflects his creation, he is evolving with us. He moves towards us as we…

POPE BENEDICT: I am the way! The truth! And the life! _Where should we find him if He is always moving_?

CARDINAL BERGOGLIO: _On the journey_.

POPE BENEDICT: This is your ego talking! You think you know better!

CARDINAL BERGOGLIO: I'm an Argentinian. How does an Argentinian kill himself? He climbs to the top of his ego and jumps off.

The joke fails to heal the POPES's irritation with BERGOGLIO.

The POPE's ASSISTANT _and a_ NUN _enter. The_ NUN _carries a_ TRAY _with two glasses of water._

BERGOGLIO _is given a glass of water by the NUN._

CARDINAL BERGOGLIO: Gracias.

The ASSISTANT _meanwhile whispers in the POPE's ear…_

POPE BENEDICT: Ah ha, Ah ha. Yes. Mmmm. _(He nods.)_ Si. Si.

The POPE, troubled, hands the FILE and his UMBRELLA to the ASSISTANT.

The POPE is then passed a glass of water by the NUN. He drinks, and then –

POPE BENEDICT: It is too hot. We should walk, further into the garden. There are parts…I have not…explored…

Starts to exit…

CADINAL BERGOGLIO: If there is some shade…

POPE BENEDICT: Yes, and perhaps we'll find God over there. "On the journey". I'll introduce you to him.

The POPE _exits._ BERGOGLIO _hands his umbrella to the assistant, then follows._

The ASSISTANT *clears away tray and file and umbrella.*

The scene now TRANSITIONS, *and we find ourselves in...*

...a WILD PART OF THE GARDEN. A loud sound of CICADAS fills this woodland...there is a clearing downstage. They walk under twisted boughs...

POPE BENEDICT: "A salesman. For a product."

CARDINAL BERGOGLIO: I simply mean –

POPE BENEDICT: We defend two thousand years of tradition. But Bergoglio knows better.

CARDINAL BERGOGLIO: We have spent these last years disciplining anyone who disagrees with our line on birth control, divorce and remarriage, being gay. While our planet was being destroyed, while inequality grew like a cancer, we worried about whether it was all right to say mass in Latin, whether girls should be allowed to be altar servers? We built a wall around ourselves and all the time the real danger was inside, inside with us.

POPE BENEDICT: What are you talking about?

CARDINAL BERGOGLIO: I think you know. We knew that there were priests ... bishops ... great men of the Church who preyed on children. And what did we do?

POPE BENEDICT: We are addressing this.

CARDINAL BERGOGLIO: We heard their confession. And moved them on to their next parish, where they could start all over again.

POPE BENEDICT: We believed if their confession...

CARDINAL BERGOGLIO: "That it was better if nine children suffer than if nine million lost their faith because of a scandal?"

67

POPE BENEDICT: No. Of course not. That's grotesque.

CARDINAL BERGOGLIO: A bishop. He said it to me.

POPE BENEDICT: How did you answer him?

CARDINAL BERGOGLIO: I told him to remove the priest from his ministry, and commission the canonical trial straight away. I did not think that a few magic words from the priest would make everything alright again.

POPE BENEDICT: "Magic words"?! Is that how you describe the sacrament of …

CARDINAL BERGOGLIO: Confession cleans the sinner's soul. It doesn't help the victim. Our whole church is in need of forgiveness. Where is our humility? Sin is _a wound_, not a stain. We need to take action to repair the wound.

POPE BENEDICT: You say "we" but you mean _I'm_ the one to blame.

CARDINAL BERGOGLIO: No, Holy Father, please.

POPE BENEDICT: Your protest – _listen to me_ – your resignation is a protest against the Holy See. And you are asking me to ratify it.

CARDINAL BERGOGLIO: No.

POPE BENEDICT: *(Fiercely.)* You say you no longer wish to be a Cardinal Archbishop. Can I ask you: are you sure you still wish to be a priest? Now, you think about that!

The POPE exits, leaving a distraught. BERGOGLIO.

BERGOGLIO moves…downstage. His MOBILE PHONE rings.

CARDINAL BERGOGLIO: Hello. Si. Tell me now. OK. But… stop…Suarez – is he? Suarez is playing? Oh thank God. On the right wing. No, I will try and watch from the airport. Ciao.

Enter SISTER BRIGITTA –

SISTER BRIGITTA: Your eminence, the Pope has invited you to stay the night.

CARDINAL BERGOGLIO: The night? But I only…need…

(Produces his resignation papers.)

SISTER BRIGITTA: A room has been prepared for your. His holiness will speak with you after dinner.

CARDINAL BERGOGLIO: After dinner?

SISTER BRIGITTA: Si.

SISTER BRIGITTA exits. BERGOGLIO is left alone, with his thoughts.

SCENE 2

Castel Gandolfo. That night. The POPE's private rooms – a TV, a couch, two armchairs, a piano. BERGOGLIO has been shown in by the ASSISTANT…

CARDINAL BERGOGLIO: Grazie.

He sees the TV, turns it on, and channel surfs until he finds FOOTBALL.

We then hear – OFF – the POPE's FITNESS WATCH: "WELL DONE. YOU DID 10,000 STEPS TODAY." Enter, the POPE…

POPE BENEDICT: Ah, ten thousand paces.

(Sees the TV.)

Football. You love football. I like it too but I've never understood the excitement myself.

CARDINAL BERGOGLIO: Really? Not even during the world cup? You know, your national team and mine…we could be in the final together. Next year. They could be – Germany – a match for Argentina.

POPE BENEDICT: *(Disinterested.)* Yeah. It's good.

Swallowing a BARLEY SUGAR. BERGOGLIO pulls out his papers –

CARDINAL BERGOGLIO: Holy Father, I want you to...look at my papers.

POPE BENEDICT: No, no, no, no, no, no.

BERGOGLIO: Please, please, this is the reason I'm here.

POPE BENEDICT: *(Firmly.)* *Nein!*

POPE BENEDICT: Please, I know you like to talk but I'm tired, I'm exhausted. I need to rest. Sit down and just be quiet together. Please sit. That's good… I get so tired. Would you like a tea or coffee?

CARDINAL BERGOGLIO: No, no. I find if I drink coffee too late at night I can't sleep.

POPE BENEDICT: Me, too…

The men sit in silence for several moments. SILENCE.

POPE BENEDICT: You know… the hardest thing is to listen, to hear his voice…God's voice.

CARDINAL BERGOGLIO: Even for a Pope?

POPE BENEDICT: Perhaps especially for a Pope.

(Beat.)

When I was young – many hundreds of years ago *(Laughs.)* – I always knew what He wanted of me – what God wanted – what purpose He had for me. But now, I don't know – perhaps I need to listen more intently. What do you think Cardinal Bergoglio?

(Pause.)

I don't know. Perhaps I need a spiritual hearing aid.

(Beat.)

Who does know? When I first heard that voice – that call – whatever that was – God's voice. It brought me peace. Such peace.

POPE BENEDICT: You must have felt that?

CARDINAL BERGOGLIO: The call yes – the peace.

(Beat.)

At 14 I realised I wanted to serve the poor. But…then there was also…other temptations.

POPE BENEDICT: Such as?

CARDINAL BERGOGLIO: I was in love.

POPE BENEDICT: With a girl?

CARDINAL BERGOGLIO: I proposed marriage to her. Amalia Damonte. I told her if she said "No", I would become a priest…

The CARDINAL holds out his arms as in "Here I am!"

CARDINAL BERGOGLIO: Also, my mother wanted me to be a doctor. She said I was too intelligent to be a priest. But I told her I want to be "a doctor of the soul." She threw a pot at me.

POPE BENEDICT: But God spoke to you. And you still hear him? Just as clearly? Mmmm? Just as strongly? You *hear* him?

BERGOGLIO nods. The POPE nods, looking wistful.

CARDINAL BERGOGLIO: But now I live in a constant state of suffering… for San Lorenzo Football Club. Ha!

The ASSISTANT enters, with WATER, and FANTA, on a tray.

POPE BENEDICT: *(To the ASSISTANT.)* Thankyou.

(To BERGOGLIO.)

Fanta? Or water?

CARDINAL BERGOGLIO: Water. Grazie. But let me –

POPE BENEDICT: No, no.

The POPE pours water for BERGOGLIO and Fanta for himself.

POPE BENEDICT: Always loved Fanta. Coca Cola was banned, you know. During the war. Fanta was allowed. Liked it ever since. Mmmm. There.

The POPE goes over to the piano to sit down.

POPE BENEDICT: Do you play?

CARDINAL BERGOGLIO: No. But I know you do. You made an album. "Music from the Vatican Alma Mater."

POPE BENEDICT: That's right, I did. Do you have a copy?

CARDINAL BERGOGLIO: Yes, yes por supuesto.

POPE BENEDICT: I could sign it for you.

CARDINAL BERGOGLIO: Yes. Please. Could you play something now?

The POPE opens the keyboard lid and sits at the piano bench.

POPE BENEDICT: Well, I'm a bit out of practice. Let's see. I'll try.

The POPE starts playing, then stops.

POPE BENEDICT: I've got this little piece by my favourite Czech…It's a lullaby. I'll see what I can do.

He continues playing. Stops again.

72

POPE BENEDICT: He lived a very tragic life, you know.

He plays the lullaby.

POPE BENEDICT: You know, the album – It was recorded at a world famous studio in London – I was told I should feel honoured because The Beatles were there – you know the Beatles?

CARDINAL BERGOGLIO: Yes. I know who they are.

POPE BENEDICT: Of course you do.

CARDINAL BERGOGLIO: Eleanor Rigby.

POPE BENEDICT: Who?

CARDINAL BERGOGLIO: Eleanor Rigby.

POPE BENEDICT: I don't know.

CARDINAL BERGOGLIO: "Yellow Submarine."

POPE BENEDICT: Sorry, I don't know…

CARDINAL BERGOGLIO: The album. Yellow submarine.

BERGOGLIO starts singing the tune.

POPE BENEDICT: Yellow submarine? That's silly. That's very funny.
I can't remember where the studio was – a church or something.

CARDINAL BERGOGLIO: Abbey Road

POPE BENEDICT: The Abbey – yes – of course.

The POPE starts playing the Schumann Traumerei.

CARDINAL BERGOGLIO: You went to Abbey Road?

POPE BENEDICT: Oh no. That would have not been appropriate.

The POPE plays quietly.

POPE BENEDICT: You know, our mother thought I had a calling for music, but my brother, he's the choir master at the cathedral in Regensburg.

The POPE stops playing and suddenly changes the rhythm to a popular German Radio song from the thirties – Fox Trot –

POPE BENEDICT: You like?

CARDINAL BERGOGLIO: It's very different! It's wonderful.

POPE BENEDICT: It's an old Berlin Cabaret song. It was made famous on the radio before the War by a singer called Zara Leander.

CARDINAL BERGOGLIO: Who?

POPE BENEDICT: Zara Leander. She was Hitler's favourite singer. She had a deep voice. She was Swedish.

CARDINAL BERGOGLIO: Sorry, who was it?

POPE BENEDICT: Zara Leander.

POPE BENEDICT: Would you like some wine? Next door.

CARDINAL BERGOGLIO: Oh, si. Grazie.

BERGOGLIO exits, then returns with a DECANTER of WINE, and a two glass.

CARDINAL BERGOGLIO: For you?

POPE BENEDICT: No, no. *(Sings.)* Dah, dah, dah, dee, dee…

As the POPE plays, both start singing the tune…

POPE BENEDICT: Good wine?

CARDINAL BERGOGLIO: Granados.

The POPE stops playing.

POPE BENEDICT: Stockhausen…

The POPE plays a naughty little slice of STOCKHAUSEN, then closes the lid of the piano.

POPE BENEDICT: I'm afraid at the keyboard, I'm not infallible. But I enjoy it.

The POPE settles down in an armchair in front of the TV.

POPE BENEDICT: *(Tired now.)* Oh well. There. I get so tired. You know?

BERGOGLIO sees his moment and produces his papers and a pen – he offers it to the POPE, who – reaches out, as if to take the PEN but then picks up, from a side table between them, the REMOTE CONTROL. He begins to channel surf.

POPE BENEDICT: You're very popular. This popularity of yours. Is there a trick to it?

CARDINAL BERGOGLIO: I try to be myself.

BERGOGLIO, frustrated, pockets his papers.

POPE BENEDICT: Hmm, when I try to be myself, people don't seem to like me very much.

(Re the TV.)

The signal. Not good today. Sometimes its good.
Sometimes bad.

The POPE surfs until he begins to close his eyes. Soon he is asleep, still holding the REMOTE CONTROL.

BERGOGLIO tries to ease it from the POPE's hand, and manages – switching the CHANNEL to FOOTBALL. But he hits the VOLUME BUTTON, and the sounds wakes up the POPE. BERGOGLIO switches off the TV.

POPE BENEDICT: I lack company. Always alone.

CARDINAL BERGOGLIO: Isiah 41.x.

POPE BENEDICT: "Do not be afraid for I will be with you." I know He's there but He doesn't laugh, you know. At least I don't hear Him laugh. You know. No, you don't know. Someone like you will never understand what I mean.

(Beat.)

I'm sorry, I must rest. It's been a long day.

He rises.

POPE BENEDICT: Oh, I've been called back to Rome. Urgent business. Something...

CARDINAL BERGOGLIO: I hope this urgent business is nothing too distressing.

POPE BENEDICT: The curia is a creature, with many arms. Able to defend itself too well. Anyway, if you would join me there. Tomorrow. We could ride the papal helicopter together.

CARDINAL BERGOGLIO: Helicopter?

POPE BENEDICT: Yes. We must leave early. We can continue our discussion, in Roma. Si?

CARDINAL BERGOGLIO: I...if...of course. As you wish, Holy Father. I was due to return to Argentina –

POPE BENEDICT: Good. The view of Rome, ancient Rome, from a helicopter, you'll enjoy it.

CARDINAL BERGOGLIO: Goodnight Holy Father.

POPE BENEDICT: Nunc dimittis. Let your servant depart in peace now Lord, according to your word...

CARDINAL BERGOGLIO: *(Joining in the prayer.)* For my eyes have seen your salvation which you have prepared for all the peoples. To be a light to lighten the world.

POPE BENEDICT: God grant us a quiet night and a perfect end. Gute Nacht.

Bergoglio goes to give him a big hug but the POPE mistakes the gesture for an incoming handshake and they end up awkwardly holding hands as if about to dance.

CARDINAL BERGOGLIO: Gute Nacht.

POPE BENEDICT: Buenas Noches.

The POPE takes a CANDLE and walks downstage, the lights dimming on the scene behind him. He moves to, what we suggest may be, a chapel, where he sets goes down on one knee and sets the candle beside him.

He prays – prays for guidance – which, to his anguish, does not come. Finally, in frustration …he snuffs out the candle with his fingers. SNAP TO BLACK.

SCENE 3

The Sistine Chapel. On the rear wall, the great fresco "The Last Judgement" by Michelangelo.

Lights slowly up on this wonder of the world, as BERGOGLIO, enters, awe-struck. He studies the LAST JUDGEMENT, until – a door opens. A figure appears. The POPE walks up to BERGOGLIO.

POPE BENEDICT: I've never been in here before…when it was empty, I mean. No visitors, no tourists. I wanted to experience the moment with you.

CARDINAL BERGOGLIO: If I was Pope I'd be in here every day.

POPE BENEDICT: What else?

CARDINAL BERGOGLIO: What?

POPE BENEDICT: If you had been chosen. What else would you do?

CARDINAL BERGOGLIO: Holy Father ...

POPE BENEDICT: This place would be different, I think.

CARDINAL BERGOGLIO: *(Pointing up at the ceiling.)* As Michelangelo shows us, Jesus was always breaking bread, feeding the people...

POPE BENEDICT: What else would you change?

CARDINAL BERGOGLIO: I'd sort out the bank.

POPE BENEDICT: Good luck with that.

CARDINAL BERGOGLIO: The banks almost destroyed my country. They beg for deregulation like tigers pleading to be let out of their cages. They devour everything in sight.

(Pointing to a new scene on the ceiling.)

And here...the only way to follow Him is to be where He is. With the people. Today where would he be? Right now? In the bomb craters in Syria. On the little beaches welcoming refugees. At Lampedusa. In hospitals...

(Referring to the chapel.)

Not here... see?... You're beginning to be glad I'm resigning.

POPE BENEDICT: For weeks, I've been praying for a sign.

CARDINAL BERGOGLIO: I don't understand.

POPE BENEDICT: When your request to resign came I knew I couldn't accept it without speaking to you. You had to come here. But perhaps you had to come here for some other purpose.

CARDINAL BERGOGLIO: Like what?

POPE BENEDICT: I have made a decision about something. A decision of great importance for the life of the whole Church. For her future. Something I ask you to hide in your soul, and speak of to no one.

(Pause.)

Sometimes you notice little things. The other night after prayers I blew out the candle. Instead of rising up, the smoke went down. Like Cain's offering. Do you notice such things?

CARDINAL BERGOGLIO: I decided to buy a ticket for my flight here before you requested my presence.

The POPE reacts with excitement to this –

POPE BENEDICT: No! Really? That gives me encouragement. You are the right person.

(Throw away.)

I'm going to resign.

CARDINAL BERGOGLIO: The right person for what?

POPE BENEDICT: To tell. I need to say it out loud to someone first.

CARDINAL BERGOGLIO: Say what?

POPE BENEDICT: What I just said. I'm going to resign.

CARDINAL BERGOGLIO: Resign from what?

POPE BENEDICT: The Papacy. The Chair of St Peter. The Bishopric of Rome. I'm going to renounce them all.

CARDINAL BERGOGLIO: But then…I mean…you can't. If you did that, you wouldn't be Pope any more.

POPE BENEDICT: Yes.

CARDINAL BERGOGLIO: But you are the Pope…

POPE BENEDICT: Yes.

CARDINAL BERGOGLIO: Popes can't resign.

POPE BENEDICT: In fact it's not without precedent. Celestine V did it in 1294.

CARDINAL BERGOGLIO: Holy Father…You think people will not be shocked because this happened once before…seven hundred years ago?!

The POPE stands.

POPE BENEDICT: The marble is too cold.

CARDINAL BERGOGLIO: I can't breathe…I came here just to ask for your signature on a piece of paper.

POPE BENEDICT: Now you know why I couldn't give you that. There will be another conclave. It is important that you are there. Eligible for election. Your future is in God's hands.

CARDINAL BERGOGLIO: But, Holy Father, you cannot do this. You *must* not! Why do the Presidents of America and Russia, of China, all come to you? Because, unlike them, your authority derives from the fact *you will suffer and die on the job*. A Pope represents service – life long – until death! – a martyr for justice and truth. For this *all* people come. Forgive me but…

POPE BENEDICT: But?

CARDINAL BERGOGLIO: … Christ did not come down from his cross.

POPE BENEDICT: God always grants you the right words.

CARDINAL BERGOGLIO: The Pope must go on, to the end. Be the personification of the crucified Christ! If you resign you will damage the prestige of the papacy forever.

POPE BENEDICT: And what damage will I do if I remain?

CARDINAL BERGOGLIO: I can't understand how this conversation is happening. The last time anyone discussed a thing like this, these frescoes weren't painted. Two Popes? Unthinkable.

POPE BENEDICT: In 1978 we had three.

CARDINAL BERGOGLIO: Not at the same time! One after the other.

POPE BENEDICT: I was making a little joke.

CARDINAL BERGOGLIO: A joke?

POPE BENEDICT: A German joke. It doesn't have to be funny.

CARDINAL BERGOGLIO: What would you be called?

POPE BENEDICT: Pope *Emeritus*.

CARDINAL BERGOGLIO: Two Popes. Both commanding authority.

POPE BENEDICT: Only one would command authority. I would hide away...out of the spot-light. Silence incarnate. *Silenzio Incarnato.*

CARDINAL BERGOGLIO: Even if you are never seen or heard again, you will still exist.

POPE BENEDICT: For a while at any rate.

CARDINAL BERGOGLIO: But your *views*, very well known views, will *exist.* And therefore will have authority still.

POPE BENEDICT: There's a saying – the Lord corrects one Pope by giving us the next. I'd like to see my correction.

CARDINAL BERGOGLIO: May I speak, Holy father?

POPE BENEDICT: Go on.

CARDINAL BERGOGLIO: For two thousand years...two thousand...the church has tried to avoid having two popes, and has almost entirely succeeded. As you know, some of your more unfortunate predecessors, your Holiness, were even poisoned so that the situation never came up. And the reason? *Infallibility.* The grace of infallibility! The gift of correctness, God's gift to he who sits in Peter's chair, the grace of being right, indisputably right, right *now* but most importantly in the future also, for time immemorial. The Pope's word is God's word undiluted. So! How could we, you and I, two Popes, *coexist,* given our differences – *and both be infallible*! – both be right?...when...when we clearly disagree on nearly everything?

POPE BENEDICT: Cardinal, as you know, Infallibility is only credited to Papal decrees on dogma when made *ex cathedra,* invoking the full authority of the Majestarium...not daily views that I, in retirement, might express. These would not be infallible.

CARDINAL BERGOGLIO: Still. Even daily views, if they differed from those of the new pope, it would cause chaos. In the case of you and I – Heaven forbid! – for every minor papal pronouncement or view there would walk and breathe the rebuttal, the living counter-argument – invalidating it. Cancelling it out! The faithful would be completely confused about whose papal position to listen to, and obey! Divisions would erupt. And then neither pope would have the authority the title of 'Pope' previously carried.

POPE BENEDICT: There are more than one religion. There are many. And they can't agree on anything. It doesn't make them all wrong.

CARDINAL BERGOGLIO: And where would you live?

POPE BENEDICT: I would keep out of your way.

CARDINAL BERGOGLIO: "My" way?! Not "my way."

POPE BENEDICT: Whoever's way.

CARDINAL BERGOGLIO: Are you being pressured to go? The Curia?

POPE BENEDICT: If there was pressure from there, I would resist it. I know my reasons are pure. I'm a scholar not a manager – I have a pace-maker and can no longer see out of my left eye. Governance requires eyes I don't have. I have fought and fought to do what needs to be done. But I have lost.

POPE BENEDICT's watch beeps: "Time to walk. Get started" The POPE stands up and starts walking.

CARDINAL BERGOGLIO: It is our weakness that calls forth the grace of God. When we offer our weakness. He gives us strength.

POPE BENEDICT: I've answered your question…Be satisfied.

CARDINAL BERGOGLIO: With respect, Holiness, it's not I who has to be satisfied. It's 1.2 billion believers. They will need to know why. There must be some extraordinary reason why…why a traditionalist like yourself would do the most un-traditional thing imaginable.

(Beat.)

Otherwise they will think there is some scandal, some plot…

POPE BENEDICT: _That_ is the calculation of leadership. A calculation we must both make.

CARDINAL BERGOGLIO: Both? Why?

POPE BENEDICT: For weeks I have been praying. I wanted to resign. But the thought that stopped me – what if at the next conclave, they voted for you.

CARDINAL BERGOGLIO: Then I offered my resignation.

POPE BENEDICT: Exactly. And I was delighted. One reason I didn't want to resign was… _what if you were next?_ And so you came. And now I've… _changed._

CARDINAL BERGOGLIO: You compromised.

POPE BENEDICT: No. I've changed. It's a different thing. Your approach, your style is radically different from mine. And I don't agree with most things you say and do…But now I can see, perhaps, a _necessity_ for Bergoglio. I cannot do this without knowing that there is at least a possibility that you might be chosen.

CARDINAL BERGOGLIO: No. Father, I could never…not me.

POPE BENEDICT: We both know, in our hearts, that it could be.

CARDINAL BERGOGLIO: If my time with you has proved anything, it has proven that you cannot go. Not unless your replacement is a second you. A second Benedict. Another Ratzinger.

POPE BENEDICT: In fact I do have a brother and we do agree on most things.

CARDINAL BERGOGLIO: Is that another German joke?
Well. Even if you do resign I cannot possibly succeed you.

POPE BENEDICT: And why not?

CARDINAL BERGOGLIO: I am a sinner. I am not worthy to lead.

POPE BENEDICT: We are all sinners. And very few ever thought me worthy.

CARDINAL BERGOGLIO: But I have sinned, *grievously*. You cannot choose me!

POPE BENEDICT: *The conclave will choose. And you may be elected.* I will not remove you from contention.

CARDINAL BERGOGLIO: I beg you! Release me! I beg you… Holy Father!

POPE BENEDICT: My son…

CARDINAL BERGOGLIO: Please! I beg you…

BERGOGLIO stuns the POPE…by getting down on his knees…and then prostrating himself, lying face-down on the ground

POPE BENEDICT: Cardinal! Please! Stop! Get up! Get up. Please.

BERGOGLIO gets back to his feet.

CARDINAL BERGOGLIO: There is a reason I cannot be chosen. We are all sinners, but I have sins that disqualify me from consideration.

POPE BENEDICT: I have finished reading your file.

CARDINAL BERGOGLIO: Then the file in not complete! It is not complete.

BERGOGLIO prepares to make his great confession –

CARDINAL BERGOGLIO: As head of the Jesuits in Argentina, I did business with the junta, that awful regime with its death squads.

The military dictatorship – tens of thousands disappeared, anyone who disagreed with their views, families destroyed, children taken from their mothers, priests working with the poor assassinated in the streets. To save the lives of my priests I needed to remain in the military's favour. When they asked, I did not deny them mass. In the home of General Videla, that tyrant, where I went to plead for the return of the stolen, I even gave communion – the body of Christ I placed on that mass-murderer's tongue. Then I took tea with him. *(Beat.)* Yes. I did this. I *made* myself do this! But I did not support their actions, attacking and disappearing and killing our people in their tens of thousands. I helped smuggled many in danger out of the country. And not one of my Jesuits died.

(Beat.)

But…at the same time…it is true…I had lost sympathy for Marxist ideology, an elite program, imposed on the poor from above, by intellectuals, with terrible consequences for the poor.

(Beat.)

So, in the name of unity, even as some Jesuits wanted to embrace armed resistance to the junta, I said "No, I forbid it."…

(In anguish.)

I forbid it…I forbid it…That is why I closed down our missions in the slums where priests and nuns were deemed by the military, a _zurdo_, a communist. I stopped our work of delivering the sacraments to the poor to protect my priests. To keep a low profile. I felt we must not provoke the junta unnecessarily or else Jesuits would also number among the dead. With our low profile we were able to hide and get out of the country dozens marked for death.

(Beat.)

Father Yorio. And Father Jalics. Two of my priests. They had been my teachers at theology school. They believed in Liberation Theology, that direct action by priests and nuns in the face of terror ought be allowed, even armed resistance, collaboration with the guerillas. They refused to leave their missions in the barios and slums. Disobeyed my orders. Refused to dissolve their communities. Did I become angry? Did I over-react to my authority being ignored? Did my judgement become clouded by my ego?

(Beat.)

In consultation with me, the Archbishop removed their right to say weekday Mass, and on Sunday they could only minister Mass in private, in their homes. I didn't doubt that I was doing the right thing. I was full of the certainty that comes with power. It was the Cold War, Marxism seemed the great enemy.

POPE BENEDICT: I have heard what you say, but there is nothing here to disqualify you from consideration. Quite the contrary. I agree with your hard stand against the Marxist-Liberation philosophy movement. I am actually encouraged by this story.

CARDINAL BERGOGLIO: May 25th, 1976.

POPE BENEDICT: What is that?

CARDINAL BERGOGLIO: 200 naval storm-troopers descended on the shanty town. Yorio and Jalics were saying Mass for the slum families. No longer enjoying the church's protection, they were taken by truck to a secret location. Tortured. For five months. Often kept naked in their cells. I used my contacts with the military to try to free them but it was useless. Useless! It was my fault.

(Beat.)

Where was Christ in the days of the dictatorship, huh?
Was he taking meetings in the presidential palace, or was
he being tortured in prisons? And where was I, huh?

POPE BENEDICT: Dictatorships take away our freedom to choose
– we both know that.

CARDINAL BERGOGLIO: I could have spoken out in public.

POPE BENEDICT: And if no-one listened, what then?

(Beat.)

But perhaps the path appears straight when we look back
at it. On the way we often feel lost...the dark night of the
soul.

CARDINAL BERGOGLIO: For my sins I was eventually removed
from office, cast out, for my failings, for my sins.

POPE BENEDICT: So.

CARDINAL BERGOGLIO: You see! It is impossible.

POPE BENEDICT: You made mistakes. But you have repented
for these, and only the person who fully repents and cleanses
themselves can understand how to bring that same sense of
peace and forgiveness to all the sinners of the world.

It helps "*to know what you are saying No to*" – yes?

CARDINAL BERGOGLIO: I am guilty, guilty of the most heinous
of sins!

POPE BENEDICT: Guilty? Perhaps. But guilt is *useful*. There is
no better agent for good behavior than guilt. Take it from
a German.

(Beat.)

Now let me tell you about the real Bergoglio, the one you are blind to. I finished reading your file this morning. So let me reveal you to *yourself.*

(Beat.)

When democracy finally returned to Argentina, you had made enemies among your fellow Jesuits. You were accused of hard line views, of being right-wing, of having sinned by doing too little, of being egotistical. Finally, your own order moved against you. 'Bergoglio has to go.' So. You were cast out, removed from your position, stripped of all authority. Your supporters were dispersed, sent abroad, told not to contact you. Finally, in shame, you were sent – to Cordoba. Exiled, to the mountains. There the exile would stay, in that little village – in that little room no bigger than a prisoner's cell – for two years.

CARDINAL BERGOGLIO: Two years.

POPE BENEDICT: Two years of introspection, of change, of dark nights, of interior crisis…

POPE BENEDICT: And in that time did *you* ask God for forgiveness?

CARDINAL BERGOGLIO: It is all I did.

POPE BENEDICT: Then perhaps you are forgiven.

BERGOGLIO shakes his head –

CARDINAL BERGOGLIO: Sin is more than a stain that can be removed by a trip to the dry cleaner. It is a *wound,* that needs to be treated, healed.

POPE BENEDICT: Then you did your best to heal and treat that wound…Your library began once more to include some books that drew surprise. "INTRODUCING LIBERATION

THEOLOGY"… "A THEOLOGY OF LIBERATION"…
"DEMOCRACY AND POLITICAL THEORY"

CARDINAL BERGOGLIO: My compliments to the Records Office.

POPE BENEDICT: Two years. Until you were noticed again. At an international gathering, you were asked to speak…

The POPE produces a transcript of BERGOGLIO's speech…

POPE BENEDICT: "*Human rights are not only violated by terrorism, repression or assassination, but also by unfair economic structures that create huge inequalities.*" Could be Karl Marx.

"*Now some people continue to defend without evidence trickle-down theories which assume that if companies at the top get wealthier the poor at the bottom will eventually enjoy the benefits. But what is trickling down, except pain and misery and stunted lives? I say this…Every community is called to be an instrument for the liberation, the liberation and…*"

POPE BENEDICT: *…the promotion of the poor!*"	CARDINAL BERGOGLIO: *… the promotion of the poor.*"

POPE BENEDICT: Could be Fathers Yorio or Jalics?

CARDINAL BERGOGLIO: This is torture.

POPE BENEDICT: Soon, you received an invitation. To be Bishop. Of Buenos Aires. You transformed yourself. Atoned. Devoted yourself to good works. I heard the stories. Transformed yourself. Renounced luxury. I heard the stories. You work in the slums yourself, the "Bishop Of The Slums"--returning to the work you once denied Fathers Yorio and Jalics.

(Pause.)

Did you…did you ever reconcile with these priests?

CARDINAL BERGOGLIO: With Yorio. Yes. We did a Mass together…We embraced, cried in each other's arms. I asked him to forgive me.

POPE BENEDICT: He forgave you?

BERGOGLIO nods – through tears. He is crying now. The POPE passes him a handkerchief.

CARDINAL BERGOGLIO: I'm sorry. It's…

POPE BENEDICT: And Jalics?

CARDINAL BERGOGLIO: Jalics? Never forgave. To the end he thought me a traitor. Among many in Argentina I am still a controversial figure.

CARDINAL BERGOGLIO: So…

POPE BENEDICT: So.

Certain his revelations have ended all thoughts of his candidacy…

CARDINAL BERGOGLIO: I am unworthy.

POPE BENEDICT: For a time you were, yes. But you changed, and began to lead, not by the example of power, but the power of example.

CARDINAL BERGOGLIO: That sinner is still inside me.

POPE BENEDICT: Then we are at an impasse. You cannot resign until I agree to your going. I cannot resign until you agree to stay. It's a conundrum.

(Beat.)

I'm just going to tell you one little thing. We all suffer from spiritual pride. We all do. You must remember that, uh… you are not God. In God we move and live and have our being. We live in God but we are not 'of' it. You're only human.

The two men look into each other's eyes.

POPE BENEDICT: But –

(Pointing up at the ceiling.)

– there he is. Human. Ja. So. If you will allow me, my son, you must believe in the mercy that you preach.

The POPE rises and stands over BERGOGLIO, with his hand outstretched over the CARDINAL's head in blessing –

POPE BENEDICT: Ego di absolvo, in nomine Patris, et Filii, et Spiritus Sancti.

CARDINAL BERGOGLIO: Thank you, Holy Father.

POPE BENEDICT: Now... let me show you a man who has _not_ changed. Who refuses to change. And hear the price he has paid. Hear _my_ confession now. I have heard yours, hear mine.

CARDINAL BERGOGLIO: Your...?

The POPE takes off his white zucchetto (small skullcap), folding it, slipping it into a pocket in his cassock...

POPE BENEDICT: Brother Carmine usually does it once a week but he is away on holiday.

CARDINAL BERGOGLIO: Your holiness?

POPE BENEDICT: Don't be afraid.

The POPE is about to kneel at the bench, using it like a pew, but BERGOGLIO stops him and helps him to sit.

CARDINAL BERGOGLIO: Your holiness, no...

POPE BENEDICT: You wouldn't deny me a confession, would you Cardinal? Begin. "In nomine Patris et Filii et Spiritus Sancti. Bless me father--for I have sinned... How long since..."

CARDINAL BERGOGLIO: How long since your last confession?

POPE BENEDICT: Oh. Seven, eight days.

CARDINAL BERGOGLIO: And have you sinned greatly in that time? I don't mean to imply that you…

POPE BENEDICT: *(Laughs.)* Of course I've sinned. Small sins. Venal sins.

(Pause.)

To God, I wish to repent for the sins of my life. As a child I failed you first--by not having the bravery to taste life. I hid away with books *(Pause.)* Then in war I joined the Hitler Youth. Every fourteen year old was ordered to. I deserted. And then, within the church, I took part in the enforcement – enforcement of the truth.

CARDINAL BERGOGLIO: Oh?

POPE BENEDICT: Yes. Rules, you see, defined my life. Books, study, learning. Obedience under the law. Is this why, as Archbishop…of Munich, I failed again?

CARDINAL BERGOGLIO: Go on…

And here, the POPE leans in closely to BERGOGLIO's ear. We do not hear the POPE's CONFESSION.

Finally, BERGOGLIO rises – deeply disturbed by what he has heard. He spends many moments contemplating things.

POPE BENEDICT: I ask for forgiveness.

But BERGOGLIO hesitates to forgive –

CARDINAL BERGOGLIO: You transferred him? From parish to parish?

POPE BENEDICT: I did not give sufficient attention to the duties assigned to this one priest.

CARDINAL BERGOGLIO: "Sufficient attention"?! On and on? Village after village?

POPE BENEDICT: Forgive me.

CARDINAL BERGOGLIO: But you knew?

POPE BENEDICT: I *should* have known! The facts were sent to me! It was placed, on my desk!

CARDINAL BERGOGLIO: So while you were enforcing the truth, the rules, you forgot to love the people you were meant to protect. *(Beat.)* You confessed…you said there was more.

POPE BENEDICT: There were others. As we now know. I didn't see its true dimensions. I should have. And our old rules, of secrecy, rules I ratified…I ask for forgiveness.

BERGOGLIO stares at the POPE – not certain how he should respond.

CARDINAL BERGOGLIO: It's here, in confession, where we are forced to look at the vastness of our failures, that we finally see the vastness of His mercy.

The POPE, grief-stricken, lowers his head – no longer expecting forgiveness. BERGOGLIO sees the POPE's pain – and moves back to him.

POPE BENEDICT: If this confession is the sole reason you wish to resign, it's even more important you stay now and heal this wound! Stay here. Complete the work you have begun!

POPE BENEDICT: Every reason I give you is never enough. Then listen again! *SILENCE*!

(Beat.)

I can sit no longer on the chair of St Peter! I can no longer hear God's voice!

POPE BENEDICT: We all have moments –

POPE BENEDICT: I can no longer hear God! I pray! I believe! But only silence! How can I reveal his Word to millions when he has removed me from his confidence?

POPE BENEDICT: But we all have that experience. Even the Lord cried out "Why have you abandoned me?"

POPE BENEDICT: No. When I was a boy I felt God's presence at my side. I have been alone my whole life, but I have never been *lonely,* until now. You wished for an "extraordinary reason" for my resignation…do you have one now?

CARDINAL BERGOGLIO: And you have told this to – ?

POPE BENEDICT: No-one. You. Just you. But today, I have heard him again.

CARDINAL BERGOGLIO: You see?

POPE BENEDICT: Speaking to me in the last voice I expected him to use – *yours.* Yours Cardinal.

CARDINAL BERGOGLIO: No.

POPE BENEDICT: I have heard him in you. In your story. In your openness. In your humanity.

(Beat.)

Forgive me.

BERGOGLIO steps toward the POPE and holds his hand out over the POPE's head.

CARDINAL BERGOGLIO: God, the father of mercies, has sent the Holy Spirit among us for the forgiveness of sins; May God grant you His pardon and peace and I absolve you of your sins. But remember, truth may be vital, but without love it is also unbearable.

(Beat.)

In the name of the Father, and of the Son, and of the Holy Spirit. Amen.

POPE BENEDICT: You have lifted a great burden from my shoulders.

CARDINAL BERGOGLIO: And you have placed a heavy one on mine.

POPE BENEDICT: A new age is coming and a new leader _will_ take over. Someone able to inspire and lead the faithful back toward the faith that has been burning 2000 years.

The GUARD enters. The POPE gestures to him, and rises.

POPE BENEDICT: Our time is up. The people wait to see this miracle of art.

(Beat.)

Your name, Cardinal. Bergoglio, it's Italian?

CARDINAL BERGOGLIO: My father was born in Italy.

POPE BENEDICT: The Romans will be overjoyed. Having a German was difficult for them.

Seeing BERGOGLIO's distress –

POPE BENEDICT: Are you all right?

CARDINAL BERGOGLIO: I am devastated.

POPE BENEDICT: You know, I have worked out why the clergy wear a white collar. Do you know why? To symbolise…that we are up to our neck in it. A little joke.

As BERGOGLIO starts to exit, the POPE stops and looks up at the ceiling.

POPE BENEDICT: Have you...have you ever tried to imagine what it would be like to wake up one morning and not believe in God?

CARDINAL BERGOGLIO: No. No.

POPE BENEDICT: You and I are made for belief. But I think of those made for unbelief. How their numbers grow.

CARDINAL BERGOGLIO: Si.

POPE BENEDICT: In New York. They have a digital sign...showing the US national debt going up, up, up. It always makes me think of the growth of *unbelief* in the West, their numbers climbing, cycling so fast on the digital sign that the right-hand numbers cannot be read, a blur! Only the column recording *thousands* can be read, slowly ticking over, less and less and less. Where there is comfort and affluence we are losing.

CARDINAL BERGOGLIO: But there is another clock. Not in New York. Ticking in Africa, South America, Asia. 150 million new Catholics in the last 7 years. Telling us it is time to act. The hunger has never been greater.

POPE BENEDICT: Then there is work for you to do, Cardinal. Give us a church for the Third Millennium, a loving one, one devoted to people. And remember Saint Francis –

CARDINAL BERGOGLIO: St Francis?

POPE BENEDICT: – in the broken-down church at San Damiano when the crucifix spoke out to him, these words... "Francis... rebuild my house, which is falling into ruins." Poor St Francis. He took it literally. Started cutting stones! Ha! So even the greatest journey can begin with a mistake.

The GUARD then enters again, holding back the CROWDS, who we can now hear (OFF).

POPE BENEDICT: *(To the GUARD.)* We disappear! Don't worry.

The POPE's FITNESS WATCH: "You did 4,000 steps. Keep going. Keep going."

CARDINAL BERGOGLIO: I will still pray you change your mind and that your fears will fade.

POPE BENEDICT: I am 86 and the work of a lifetime begins now. Ha.

(Smiles.)

Remember Cardinal –

(Pointing to himself.)

Silenzio incarnato.

(Beat.)

You will be pleased to go home I expect?

CARDINAL BERGOGLIO: Speaking English is exhausting.

POPE BENEDICT: *(Nods.)* _Terrible_ language. So many exceptions to every rule. I will go out this way. You must risk the crowds I'm afraid.

CARDINAL BERGOGLIO: Oh, I'm invisible.

POPE BENEDICT: For now. For now.

It is time to part.

CARDINAL BERGOGLIO: Holy Father…

step forward to say goodbye. The POPE offers his hand but BERGOGLIO is having none of this, stepping into a hug.

CARDINAL BERGOGLIO: No, please, please, ha! Ha!

They step back, holding hands…

CARDINAL BERGOGLIO: You know St Francis he loved to dance.

POPE BENEDICT: Oh yes?

CARDINAL BERGOGLIO: He would have learnt the tango.

POPE BENEDICT: Oh, it's too late for me.

CARDINAL BERGOGLIO: Oh, no, no, no, I'll show you.

POPE BENEDICT: No, no, no, no... BERGOGLIO: Come come come come, I show you, no try, I teach you.

POPE BENEDICT: I can't dance.

CARDINAL BERGOGLIO: Now, see I go forward with my right and you go forward with your left...

UP WITH: Sound of the Berlin cabaret song, sung by Zara Leander. They laugh as BERGOGLIO tries to teach the awkward but laughing POPE how to tango. As they struggle...

CARDINAL BERGOGLIO: One, two, three, to the side, to the side. Unos, duo, tres...Ha!Ha!Ha!

POPE BENEDICT: Ha! Ha! No, no...

They cease the attempt.

POPE BENEDICT: Go, go now.

The POPE now initiates the final embrace.

POPE BENEDICT: Well my friend. Auf Wiedersehen.

CARDINAL BERGOGLIO: Auf Wiedersehen.

The POPE walks away first, a lonely figure, as the sound of the PEOPLE rises.

EPILOGUE

The ROOM OF TEARS, St Peter's Basilica. The ROOM fills with WHITE SMOKE. We also hear the hubbub, outside, of a vast CROWD, of the thousands gathered in the square. Guarding the doors to the balcony are two SWISS GUARDS.

THREE sets of PAPAL ROBES, of three different sizes, and FIVE sets of RED SHOES, await the new pope.

– Enter the new POPE FRANCIS, stepping into a bolt of heavenly light from above. He addresses the AUDIENCE.

POPE FRANCIS: Everyone was surprised that I chose to call myself 'Francis' because being Argentine, people thought I would call myself 'Jesus II'!

Enter BERGOGLIO, *the new* POPE FRANCIS *(wearing the* SCARLET ROBES *of a* CARDINAL*)...with* SISTER SOPHIA *and* SISTER BRIGITTA...

Enter, the PROTODEACON *(Cardinal Jean Louis Tauran)...*

SISTER BRIGITTA: We should try on the Mozetta *(robes).*

SISTER BRIGITTA *and* SISTER SOPHIA *wait to dress the new POPE...*

SISTER SOPHIA: You must...must choose, your holiness.

POPE FRANCIS: Nothing. I will wear what I am wearing. Thank you.

Meanwhile, we hear (off-stage, from the balcony) PROTODEACON *addressing the crowds in St Peter's Square...*

PROTODEACON *(OFF.)*: Fratelli e sorelle carissimi *(Italian) (The crowd roars.)*

Queridísimos hermanos y hermanas. *(Spanish) (The crowd roars.)*

Bien chers frères et sœurs. *(French) (The crowd roars.)*

Liebe Brüder und Schwestern. *(German) (The crowd roars.)*

Queridos irmãos e irmãs *(Portugese) (The crowd roars.)*

Ndugu na dada wapendwa *(Swahili) (The crowd roars.)*

Agapitoí adelfoí kai adelfés *(Greek) (The crowd roars.)*

Qin'ài de xiongdì jiemèimen *(Chinese)* Dear brothers and sisters.

I announce to you a great joy. Annuntio vobis gaudium magnum: HABEMUS...PAPAM!

(The crowd roars.)

WE HAVE...A POPE! THE LORD JORGE MARIO, CARDINAL BERGOGLIO, WHO HAS TAKEN THE NAME...FRANCIS.

During this –

SISTER SOPHIA: But –

POPE FRANCIS: Please. Thankyou.

SISTER SOPHIA: And the shoes? At least the red shoes.

POPE FRANCIS: My own are not worn out. Thank you for your assistance.

SISTER SOPHIA: Black shoes?!

POPE FRANCIS: Si.

He will wear what he is wearing already...simple BLACK SHOES.

POPE FRANCIS: Where are all the other cardinals?

SISTER SOPHIA looks to the more knowledgeable SISTER BRIGITTA.

SISTER BRIGITTA: Holy Father…they wish to leave you alone, in keeping with the tradition of the Pope Emeritus.

POPE FRANCIS: After I go out there, face the people, speak to them, I don't want to be alone. Invite all the cardinals. I want company. We must feed them. Do we have any food?

SISTER BRIGITTA: Food?

POPE FRANCIS: There must be food here.

SISTER BRIGITTA: Your eminence, this is the Vatican.

POPE FRANCIS: Go find out if we have food please.

SISTER BRIGITTA nods to SISTER SOPHIA, who exits…

POPE FRANCIS: And how am I getting home? Afterwards?

SISTER BRIGITTA: You are home, Holy Father.

POPE FRANCIS: Am I? I…would like to sleep tonight in my old room. Like the other Cardinals, at the Hotel Santa Marta.

SISTER BRIGITTA: Your Holiness. That is not possible. You are Pope.

POPE FRANCIS: Never mind that. I want to be driven to Casa Santa Marta.

SISTER BRIGITTA: I shall arrange the limousine.

POPE FRANCIS: No, no, no, no. I will go with the other Cardinals.

SISTER BRIGITTA: In…in the…?

POPE FRANCIS: The Mini-van. Si. You can say it. The *Mini-van.*

SISTER BRIGITTA: The Mini-van.

POPE FRANCIS: There! It didn't hurt you.

Enter SISTER SOPHIA –

SISTER SOPHIA: Holy Father –

POPE FRANCIS: What news?

SISTER SOPHIA: We have ice-cream. Vanilla.

POPE FRANCIS: They will be delighted. Ice-cream for all. Ice-cream it is. *Habeas Vanilla.*

As he turns and faces the doors to the balcony and takes a couple of steps toward them, then turns back to the NUNS and says.

POPE FRANCIS: Pray for me. A sinner.

He now, slowly, nervously, walks toward the DOORS TO THE BALCONY, and as he pushes them open himself...he becomes SATURATED in heavenly light.

We hear the sound of the tens of thousands in ST PETERS SQUARE, roaring, and under this, rising, we hear the following football commentary...

ENGLISH SPORTS COMMENTATOR *(OFF.)*: *...Schuller...Play quickens every time he's on the ball...and he's found a cross...and here's Mario Gotze!*

SPANISH SPORTS COMMENTATOR *(OFF.)*: *Goalllllllllllllllllllllll... Goalllllllllllllllllll...Goalllllllllllllllllll*

As MUSIC CRESCENDOES...

SISTER BRIGITTA and SISTER SOPHIA all bow deeply, as the DOORS TO THE BALCONY close.

And now we are back in the SISTINE CHAPEL...

Enter... THREE REFUGEES (from Africa, Syria, etc.)...who move downstage and stare in wonder at the beauty of the art of Michelangelo and of this place.

Enter...POPE FRANCIS with THREE MORE REFUGEES...

As MUSIC plays, POPE FRANCIS shows the REFUGEES the glorious art, pointing here and there, explaining this wonder of the church and the world...to the people.

Over this we hear the recorded voice of BERGOGLIO...

BERGOGLIO *(RECORDED.)*: *"Capitalism is a system of trickle down suffering. We all have to think about how we can become a little poorer."*

"Women in the church are more important than bishops and priests. The feminine genius is needed wherever we make important decisions."

"World governments are to blame for their sinful protection of those who are wounding Mother Earth, destroying our collective home."

"It is not the church's role to judge homosexuals. The Pope loves you like this."

"Abusive priests are tools of Satan...child sex abuse reminds me of the ancient practice of human sacrifice. The Church must eradicate this evil forever."

"I believe in God, not in a Catholic God, there is no Catholic God." "A hell doesn't exist."

"I see clearly that the thing the church needs most today is the ability to heal wounds and to warm the hearts of the faithful ... I see the church as a field hospital after battle."

"I ask you to pray for me, so that I too, in the field in which God has placed me, may play honestly and courageously for the good of all."

CURTAIN

Printed in the USA
CPSIA information can be obtained
at www.ICGtesting.com
LVHW020854171024
794056LV00002B/539

9 781786 827869